Strategic Airline Management

'The Global War Begins'

Louis Gialloreto

Pitman

PITMAN PUBLISHING
128 Long Acre, London, WC2E 9AN

© Louis Gialloreto 1988

First published in Great Britain 1988

British Library Cataloguing in Publication Data

Gialloreto, Louis
    Strategic airline management: the global war
    begins
    1. Airlines. Management
    I. Title
    387.7'068

ISBN 0 273 02866 9

Printed in Great Britain at The Bath Press, Avon

I would like to dedicate this book to my wife and family whose unwavering support has proved invaluable to me in this and all of my projects in life.

L.G.

Contents

4 The globalization of the air transport industry 152
The global picture · International carrier types · Carrier types and development · The US scenario · Strategic snapshot: American Airlines · The international scenario · The international future of air transportation

5 Strategic management applications 188
Strategic basics · Diagnostics generics · Environmental modelling · Airline asset acquisition · The golden rules

6 Conclusions 200

Acknowledgements

Many people have had a stake in helping me undertake a project of this magnitude. Original development of the type 1, 2, 3 carrier concept for the US marketplace was done with Dr Roger Bennett of McGill University in Montreal, who has been a source of both inspiration and challenge, in addition to being a valued friend. Keith McMullan, Editor of *The Avmark Aviation Economist*, has shown an incredible aptitude for understanding not only air transportation issues but my often unintelligible scrawl. Keith's support and friendship over the years as well as his generous and expert help in this venture were essential to its final outcome and are deeply appreciated. Andrew Hofton of the Cranfield Institute of Technology in England, whose gentle prodding to produce this book was instrumental in my deciding to do so, is one of the most knowledgeable air transport people I have had the privilege to know. During the course of my 14 year association with air transportation I have had the good fortune to have worked with or be taught by a number of very skilled people. These people include Dr N Matte and his talented faculty members at the Institute of Air & Space Law at McGill University, Mr J Landry of of the ATA in Washington DC, my former co-workers at Sypher Consulting in Ottawa, Mr K Miller, formerly of Eastern Provincial Airways, and many others who I have been fortunate to know and learn from. I conclude with special thanks to a group of people to whom I am indebted and these are my many colleagues at Air Canada. As a proud member of the Air Canada family I have been fortunate to associate with understanding superiors and peers who have continued to reinforce my interest and enthusiasm in what has to be the most exciting industry on earth, air transportation. Of course it goes without saying that this project would never have gotten off the ground, so to speak, had it not been for the support of Simon Lake and his colleagues at Pitman Publishing. I am grateful for all their help and support. Finally, I thank the people and environs of Vermont for providing me with one of the nicest and most serene environments in which to write a book.
L.G.

1 A historical perspective

'The boring thing about history is, of course, that it tends to repeat itself...'   19th Century, Anonymous

While this book's main purpose will be to deal with the evolution of business thinking in air transportation and to project future industry strategies and their consequences, I felt it important to go backwards for the purpose of rediscovery. It is not my intention, however, to discuss technical marvels, or the great spirit of aviation pioneers, as this has been ably done in other books. I would begin by concentrating, instead, on a concise review of past business trends in air transport. This will serve to re-expose some concepts that few may realize have been with us since the 1930s or before, as well as to provide a base for analysing the dynamism and cyclicality we are seeing in today's global air transportation market.

In adopting the persona of the marketer one could try to explain the beginnings of air transport as it relates to a customer need. Someone must have had a need in order for so many to have gone to such trouble and expense to develop the air transport system we know today. Back in the earliest days the prime rationale for aviation was military advantage. Concentrating on the civil side of aviation we find that time and speed were the prime rationale for the development of civil aviation. In the early days the perceived need for speed in travel and communications was not developed in the consumer's mind. In fact one could go so far as to say that in its inceptive stages air transportation did not so much fill an existing consumer need as try to create one. In fact, the development of the business of air travel revolved around the saving of time even though consumers had to be conditioned to place emphasis on saving travel time. One must remember that in the early days air transportation was not perceived as a viable business but simply as another one of those new ideas that few accepted as prudent, let alone part of any nation's public transportation system.

'It stands to reason that a means by which you gain a useful morning in London and arrive unjaded in Paris in time to pay an important business call, or with leisure time to do a little sightseeing before dinner, is worthy of some consideration.' (Adverstising booklet for London–Paris daily noontime flights, 1920)

'What's the use of getting there quicker if you haven't got anything better to say when you arrive?' (US President Calvin Coolidge, 1923)

The foregoing quotes illustrate several things. First, the basic question of whether the additional speed was indeed a necessary component in the public transport system. The slower transportation methods such as rail, road and ship gave people plenty of time to think and reflect before arriving at an important meeting or other function.

Air transport had not proved itself the reliable and efficient method of conveyance we know today, which meant that potential passengers had also to consider personal survival as a factor in their mode of transportation decision. The second consideration is the greater early importance placed on air transportation in Europe when compared to the U.S.. Despite the fact that the first commercial service occured in the U.S. the industry took-off, so to speak, in Europe at a much faster pace.

The first airline service began operations between St Petersburgh and Tampa, Florida, in January 1914. The 18-mile trip cost $5 each way or 28¢/mile. (In 1982, People Express flew Boston–Washington, DC, a distance of 429 miles, for $19 (off-peak) or 4.4¢/mile.) The St Petersburgh Airboat Line, despite a perfect safety record, carried 1200 passengers and folded in the spring of 1914; it was not revived. It was not only the first example of an airline but also of the demise of one because of seasonal fluctuations. The highly seasonal Florida market pulled the rug out from under the Airboat Line because they failed to realize that by starting operations in the winter peak season, traffic could only drop in the summer period. Even today, while airlines have discovered seasonality, they pay only passing heed to the potentially critical impacts of the general economic cycle on their future performance and strategies. Also of note is the fact that the US air transport industry was born in 1914 in a domestic environment devoid of economic regulation. This might lead one to surmise that Dr Kahn, the so-called father of deregulation, was merely re-inventing the deregulatory wheel in 1978.

At the close of World War I in 1918, the belligerent powers on both sides of the Atlantic Ocean found themselves with an abundance of aircraft (war surplus) and trained pilots eager to fly them for peacetime purposes. In America, where a fast and efficient railroad system spanned the nation, there was little serious interest in the aircraft as a means of transportation. Europe presented a different story. The War had wrecked much of the rail network and at the same time had acquainted Europeans at first hand with the airplane's potential. There were many heavily travelled routes that railroads could not serve, notably those over water, such as Paris–London [1].

Early passenger air transportation ventures were rarely successful (in the US). The reason was that aircraft, in terms of safety, speed and range, could barely compete with ground transportation. Consequently successful air passenger service was usually between islands and the US mainland where early aircraft competed with boats [2].

In fact in Europe the Germans, French, British, Dutch, Swiss and Belgians, had all become involved into civil air transportation by 1922. One of the interesting early air battles was the Anglo-French civil air battle on the London–Paris route. The British, who started things off on the London–Paris route, charged a £42 one-way fare (which using the £1/US $5 conversion rate at the time) came to $210.00 or $1/mile. The British carriers at the time were not government subsidized and therefore one could argue that the $210 one-way fare was the fully allocated cost of the trip. The fact that this £42 fare represented more than an average annual UK worker's salary at the time meant that access to air travel was, to say the least, restricted to the upwardly mobile. Ask no more why air travel in Europe is more expensive than even a pre-deregulated US air transport system was. Amusingly, the £42 one-way London–Paris fare was considered a no-frills fare. In 1919, Handley–Page Transport using converted bombers flew London–Paris and London–Brussels and pioneered food service to its passengers by offering lunch baskets for 3 shillings extra! [3].

Many of us thought Freddy Laker and the late People Express were so innovative with their no-frills travel concept when in fact it seems that the low service market niche was one of the original segments in air transport marketing.

The French competition helped to illustrate another air carrier concept that is still around today, although its days may be numbered in many countries. The competing French carriers on the London–Paris route were all subsidized by the French government because the French thought that the maintenance of such a service was a matter of national honour. Today, we call these types of airlines flag carriers and their survival is based on mainly political, as opposed to commercial, rationale although this is changing.

Upon seeing the easier time that the French had in financing their operations, the UK carrier complained that competition between flag carriers and private enterprise carriers was not equitable since the flag carriers could use government money to finance losses generated by competitive pressures. In 1919 and 1920 these pleas fell upon deaf UK political ears; satsified as they may have been, passengers were nonetheless not plentiful enough to make operations profitable, as the airline learned to its chagrin. All the pioneer lines lost money [4].'

A quote from a man who was to go on to greater things during the Second World war decreed that his country's struggling aviation industry 'must fly by itself; the government cannot possibly hold it up in the air'. Winston Churchill, who then held the junior government portfolio of Secretary of State for Air, could not have known that the air transport industry in the UK would have come full circle to be privately owned by 1987. In the interim, however, his political rhetoric held the airlines at bay until 1921 when: 'all of the British lines suspended service, resuming only when the government relented and offered modest subsidies to help them to meet their expenses [5].'

Secure in the knowledge that these subsidies offered something of a financial cushion, some UK carriers began experimenting with product concepts that are familiar to us today. Daimler Airlines quickly made a name for itself by striving for efficiency and improved market presence through increased frequency. Daimler planned to have as many as seven aircraft in the air at a time (its entire fleet in 1922). Relying on the theory that the difference between flying machines and aircraft is that the former make money by flying while the latter lose money sitting in hangars, we can begin to explain Daimler's drive for more efficiency. At this time the French found that they were at a disadvantage on the London–Paris route because they only flew four times a week while the UK carriers flew daily. Thus the instigation of the first recorded instance of copy-cat airline marketing by the French who went to daily service despite the fact that there was not the demand. Their additional losses were covered by the French government, prompting more complaints by UK carriers to their government. It was at this juncture, in 1922, that the UK government decided that it was difficult to compete with the stronger French airlines that were receiving strong government support.

This resulted in the creation of Imperial Airways as the British government's 'chosen instrument' for developing air transport. It was privileged as regards air subsidies; but was to use its best endeavours to make its services self-supporting at the earliest moment [6].'

The road to genuine profit for a UK government-owned carrier only started after the UK government wrote off a sizeable debt accumulated by British Airways and its predecessor carriers to start BA on the road to privatization in the early 1980s. A key change of strategy during 1922–3 was the amalgamation of many smaller carriers into a single government-owned airline in each of the European countries. There were several reasons for this phenomenon, including the fact that private carriers could not compete against stronger national carriers with their government-financing mechanisms. Additionally, these new flag carriers were just part of large infrastructural investment programmes by European governments that sought to develop an overall air transport system. Many European countries, such as Holland, the UK and France, also used their airlines as a method of maintaining better links with their colonial possessions.

The European air carrier amalgamation now projected for the late 1980s would be the second occurrence of this phenomenon, the first having transpired in the mid-1920s. In the second wave of the 1980s, the government-owned flag carriers, originally formed from the amalgamated carriers of the 1920s and 1930s, would become privatized and recombined into private cross-national and transnational carriers. Such amalgamations as Junkers Luftverkehr and Deutscher Aero Lloyd forming Lufthansa; Daimler, Handley Page, Instone and British Marine Air merging into Imperial Airways (forerunner of British Airways); five carriers amalgamating into Air France are but several examples of the 1920–30 trend towards amalgamation. In a way the European flag carrier amalgamation of the late 1980s seems a natural historical evolution following from the early days of air transport development in Europe.

During this early period in the US, the only willing passenger on the nation's domestic air transport system seemed to be the mail. By 1930 passenger air carriers had developed in such distant lands as Japan, Colombia, Australia, Russia, Mexico and several other Eastern European nations, and yet the importance of passenger air travel in the US was limited. Early conditions for passenger travel are illustrated in the trip of one James Reddig, travelling between Boston and New York in the spring of 1927 on Colonial Air Transport, a forerunner of American Airlines. Colonial was an airmail carrier, but was trying a two-week passenger carrying experiment. The fare was $25.00 one-way and Reddig was the first paying passenger in 11 days. After flying to New York, it is amusing to hear what happened:

At Hadley Field, near New Brunswick, New Jersey, where the flight terminated, Reddig got another surprise: there was no provision for ground transportation to New York. He hitched a ride in a mail truck to the New Brunswick train station, where, he had been assured New York-bound trains came through at least once an hour. Unfortunately, few of them bothered to stop at New Brunswick, and in the end it took Reddig longer to get from Hadley to New York than it had taken him to fly from Boston to Hadley [7].

This example seems to illustrate several things. First, airports were far from city centre locations even then; second, ground links to/from airports are sometimes inefficient; and third, on short distances intermodal competition is a definite consideration. It also shows that in the same period the air transport infrastructure had developed to a greater extent in Europe than it had in the US. A major early problem in the US was the safety issue. Whereas today we talk about congestion and near misses, then the topic was different. Just getting there more often than not was a major problem.

In addition to souring the public on air travel, the accidents turned the financial community against investments in airline enterprises [8].

Given the general unreliability of aircraft at the time and the lack of interest on the part of the government and the public, it could hardly have been otherwise. As the European experience had demonstrated, an airline could not exist for long without government support, but no subsidies were forthcoming from Washington. Most Americans remained sceptical about air travel; trains, while not as fast as planes on long haul runs in the late 1920s, were much safer. European governments have supported commercial aviation for reasons of national prestige, but in American politics 'subsidy' was a dirty word [9].

Or was subsidy a dirty word? The struggle to try and maintain a relatively deregulated industry while ensuring there was an industry at all proved a unique conundrum for the US. One of the turning points occurred in 1925 with the introduction of the Kelly Air Mail Act.

The Post Office operated the mail flights, government paid for and operated, until 1924 in spite of protests from the railways in the early 1920s regarding government supported competition in the transportation of mail. As a result of these protests, the Air Mail Act of 1925 (Kelly Act) was passed to encourage commercial aviation and to transfer the air mail operation to private carriers on the basis of competitive bids [10].

The Kelly Act in effect, inaugurated commercial air transportation in the US... at the time, because of the high cost of service and a relative scarcity of passengers, regular passenger air service had not yet become economically feasible [11].

So, in fact, the US government did grant subsidies to mail carriers although this did not lead to the creation of a US flag carrier. After the fledgling air carriers were given airmail contracts by the government they were still operating on rather shaky financial grounds, but they were private companies in contrast to the European scenario of heavy government involvement. Since they were private companies they were also vulnerable to takeover or partial buy-out attempts. Since the transportation powers of the day were railways, it seemed natural that they try to takeover these airmail airlines to consolidate their airmail carrying business. This is exactly what happened. Obviously the application of antitrust legislation on air transport was as effective in 1920 as it is today. The government saw that the railways would perform a cross-subsidization function to get these new mail air carriers off the ground which meant the government didn't have to.

Initially the [mail] contracts were awarded for four year periods. Under the competitive bidding system, the most significant contracts were awarded to Boeing Air Transport for the San Francisco–Chicago route and to National Air Transport for the New York–Chicago route. The transcontinental route was joined by about a dozen feeder routes, with the result that almost every major city had air mail services [12].

Thus the postal service, by its policies and procedures with respect to the letting of airmail contracts, to a great extent controlled the growth of and, in effect, 'regulated' the commercial air carriers [13].

It is worth noting that the *de-facto* regulation applied to mail only, not passenger travel. Despite this, it is true that passenger travel depended heavily on the cross-subsidization effect of mail contract revenues. Despite the additional revenues generated by airmail contracts, 'the main problem during this period was that the mail revenues were too low to justify capital expense for better equipment. Poor equipment also resulted in poor service, which in turn led to even lower revenues [14].

This was to change in the late 1920s due to a number of factors, including 'the Air Commerce Act of 1926 which initiated the development of civil airways, navigational aids and provided for the regulation of safety by the federal government [15]' This was in contrast to parallel developments in Europe where the carriers themselves paid for the infrastructural development costs. Of course the European carriers were government-owned so the difference may be marginal. It seems that governments did end up paying for development of the air system through a variety of subsidies regardless of the continent. A second factor that improved the financial viability of the industry was the extension on government mail contracts from 4 to 10 years which guaranteed funds for expansion and development. The payments for mail carriage were also made on the basis of cargo space available and distance flown as opposed to the flat rate per piece system used previously. This encouraged carriers to use larger planes and fly them longer distances, which in turn led to transcontinental flights. Since the government payments covered costs plus a marginal return, the carriage of passengers became attractive since the money generated from this activity would be purely incremental. Subsequently, the government of the day determined that carrier development was too slow. As a result the open competition bidding system used to award mail contracts was abolished in favour of one which granted exclusive 10–year route licences to the carrier who could prove that they had been serving that route for at least 6 months and would bid the lowest amount on the contract. The ability to prove that the route licence would have a positive synergistic effect on the carrier's existing route network was also a positive factor in contract awards. Putting together these main criteria, it became easy to see that new mail contract awards favoured the larger, better established carriers.

Not only was this the temporary extinguishing of open competition, but this system also provided a route award system not at all dissimilar to the one the Civil Aeronautics Board was to use in the subsequent 30- or 40-year period. The type of activity that the new policies portended actually occurred. Smaller carriers, who were unable to mount the lowest bid for new mail contracts, fell victim to a consolidation of the biggest carriers.

It is even alleged that in those cases when a contract was given to a larger carrier instead of a smaller one, the larger carrier was *obligated* to buy out the smaller carrier at a fair price. While this had the effect of strengthening the larger carriers, it could seem to the casual observer a trifle anti-competitive. Of course the rash of merger fever in the US market of the mid-1980s, while carried out under a different set of economic rules, seems to be having a similar effect and the US government seems content that these activities are not anti-competitive, just free market forces at work. Whatever the country and whatever the set of economic rules, the global trend in the late 1920s and 1930s was air carrier rationalization. In the US, the 1930s brought a mass of mergers and amalgamations with six carriers merging into United (this included Boeing Air Transport), thirteen carriers merging into American Airlines and five other carriers joining to form TWA. At that time it was becoming obvious that in order to survive in the highly competitive intermodal transport battle (rail and sea versus air travel), air carriers had to get bigger in order to sustain the high cost burden in the face of limited public acceptance and resultant low revenues.

All of the early business experience pointed out several key factors that still predominate in air transportation today, namely:

1. The provision of air transportation is an expensive, capital-intensive business. The ability to secure a steady and predictable long-term stream of revenues to help absorb these costs in an orderly and timely fashion was and still is very difficult.

2. No matter what country or government, some intervention and form of subsidy has always been present in the system, whether it was direct or indirect. Airlines have simply not been able to absorb the entire cost of operating the air transport system.

3. Many of the early marketing tactics and types of air carrier structure are still in evidence today.

4. By 1926 the UK had already experimented with deregulation and opted for subsidization and regulation.

Returning to the evolving US scenario, we note that by 1934 a new Air Mail Act had been passed. The main reason for a new Act was that by 1933 only three favoured carriers had emerged as major airmail carriers and that this had been deemed anti-competitive. Therefore the US began feeling in 1934 much the same as it was to feel in 1976–7 prior to the re-deregulation of 1978. The new 1934 Act set up a revised three-tiered regulatory system that involved the Post Office for awarding contracts, the Interstate Commerce Commission to set charges at 'fair and reasonable rates for the transportation of mail', and the Bureau of Air Commerce (forerunner of the FAA) that was to be put in charge of developing the air transport infrastructure. More interestingly, the Air Mail Act of 1934 (Black–McKeller) established two classes of air carrier, the subsidized and the unsubsidized:

[the 1934 Act]... still allowed routes to be established freely by non-subsidized airlines, since only those with mail contracts were regulated [passenger travel was becoming more and more profitable as a separate venture]. If such non-subsidized carriers established a competitive route, this lowered the passenger and express revenue of the subsidized carrier and consequently damaged its financial position. Also, some of the subsidized airlines established off-line, uneconomical and supposedly unsubsidized routes. Since any carrier could fly any route these problems were widespread [15].

The Air Mail Act of 1935 began to remedy the competitive problem this partially deregulating environment was causing. It prohibited off-line routes to any subsidized carrier. The act also disallowed losses incurred on new-mail schedules and routes [16]. This effectively united the rules among subsidized carriers, but the war still raged between the two classes of carrier: 'the mail carriers were apprehensive of this potential competition and, as a consequence, then, as now they favoured governmental control of exit/entry of new routes [17].'

This would clearly lead to the conclusion that very little in the US market had changed between 1934–5 and 1977–8. In both instances the big boys wanted their market franchise protected while the smaller new entrant carriers espoused competition as the only viable way for them to survive and flourish. So between 1934/5 and 1938 it is clear that passenger air travel had been deregulated. In 1938, however, the US government passed the Civil Aeronautics Act which:

placed the development, regulation and control of air carriers under the jurisdiction of a single, independent administrative body, the Civil Aeronautics Authority (later the Civil Aeronautics Board, CAB). This Act broadened the scope of safety regulation and for the first time subjected airlines, *all the airlines*, to economic regulation. The carriers received certificates of public convenience and necessity, specifying points to be served. Mail contracts were abolished with mail being carried by the certificated carrier on each route. The Board also exercised complete power to determine 'fair and reasonable' rates for the transportation of passengers, property and mail. The Board also had the power to regulate competition, two apparently antithetical terms. Consolidations, mergers, and acquisitions were also regulated; conflict of interest and anti-trust applications (immunity) were also given to the Board [18].

A grandfather clause sought to preserve the entrenched rights of existing large and small carriers, meaning that the air system moved from deregulation to regulation virtually intact.

As time went on, during the period from 1938 to 1978 the CAB, as empowered under the Civil Aeronautics Act and the 1958 Federal Aviation Act, continued to gain power, thus reducing the commercial freedom of market participants. Soon the rule became competition if necessary but not necessarily competition as witnessed by the following exerpt from a CAB licence hearing in the post-1950s period:

In the Miami–Los Angeles Nonstop [route] case the Board [CAB] enumerated ten different factors it had weighed in determining which, among multiple applicants, should or should not receive certificated authority to serve a particular market:

1 route integration as evidenced by the ability to convenience beyond segment traffic;
2 frequencies to be operated over the involved segment;
3 the type of equipment to be employed;
4 the fares to be charged;
5 the identity of the involved points;
6 the historic participation in the involved traffic;
7 the efforts to promote and develop the involved market;
8 the need of the applicant for route strengthening;
9 the profitability of the route for the applicants and the existing carriers;
10 the potential diversion of traffic from existing carriers.

If one believes that it was the job of the CAB to protect consumers, it should be noted that only the first four criteria would be involved in consumer protection. The latter six seek more to reduce, or minimize, competition, and to a great extent protect the incumbent market players. As a result, US carriers had to become very adept at blocking the initiative of other carriers as opposed to developing their own. There was, however, a predictability in the scheme of things and in fact a 1941 set of route award criteria seemed to speak with the same tone:

the CAB stated that four questions were to be considered in any application for new service:

1 Will the new service serve a useful public service, responsive to a public need?
2 Can and will the service be served adequately by existing routes or carriers?
3 Can the new service be served by the applicant without impairing the operations of existing carriers contrary to public interest?
4 Will any cost of the proposed service to the government be outweighed by the benefit which will accrue to the public from the new service?

Once again there is a hint of non-competitiveness in the rules of new route exit/entry or capacity increase in an existing market. As a

TABLE 1.1 CAB transition to a fixed state

	Phase I	Phase II	Phase III	Phase IV
	1938	1944	1955	1973
Environment	Momentum of other moves to regulate. Fear of cut-throat competition	Reluctant local airline experiment. Many ex-Second World War pilots and aircraft		Recognition that intrastate airlines could offer cheaper service than CAB-regulated airlines. Move to deregulate
CAB characteristics	Balance between subsidy and fare levels	Increasing requirement for CAB decisions as airlines expand force CAB to adopt generalized solutions	Need for fares policy recognized with decreasing importance of subsidy. Use of ROI leads to excess capacity through service competition	Rules set for industry aimed on cost control with limitations on capacity
Airline interface	Individually negotiated subsidy. Keep the weak in the system	Increasing importance of fare levels with trunks. Increasing importance of subsidy with locals	Pressure on higher fares tempered by fear of renewed investigation and stricter rules	Single rule for all non-subsidized airlines. More uniform treatment of subsidized airlines

Source: Airline Deregulation, The Early Experience (Meyer, Oster, Morgan, Berman, Strassman)

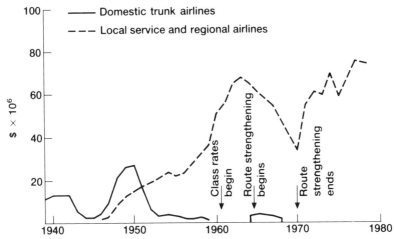

Figure 1.1   **Subsidies received by certificated carriers, 1938–78**
Source: Airline Deregulation, The Early Experience
(Meyer, Oster, Morgan, Berman, Strassman)

result, many of the early managers in air transportation were weaned on the idea that growth was a slow painful process and that any product ideas that deviated from the norm in terms of value (price for service ratio) were unlikely to be accepted and that pleasing the regulators was more important than pleasing consumers, many of whom had a limited competitive choice in many markets anyway. See Table 1.1 and Fig. 1.1.

The fact that the US air transport manager had little commercial flexibility was of negligible consequence because most of the industry's efforts and therefore most of the change and advancement were coming in the technical as opposed to commercial or managerial areas. Rapid technical development took us from the prop to the turbo prop, to the pure jet to the turbojet, and finally to the widebody turbofan with a limited venture into supersonic air transport. Once the early 1970s had passed, most of the significant technical advancement was complete. The biggest size that was likely to be needed for a while had been built, the fastest airplane had been sold to two airlines and was currently being deployed in limited fashion on particular routes, and the altitude and range requirements of existing types were thought more or less adequate until the late 1980s or early 1990s. In fact, most of the recent technical advancement has emphasized quieter, more fuel-efficient aircraft conditioned by several oil crises and heightened community sensitivity to noise. As the industry progressed through the 1960–75 period, quantum

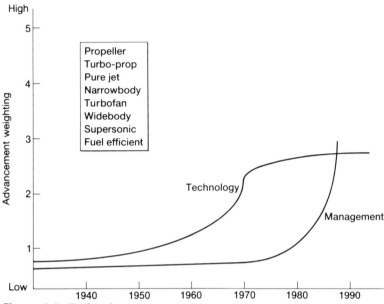

Figure 1.2 **Technology vs management innovation in air transportation**

leaps in efficiency and productivity were gained simply by purchasing new technology. Just as the pace of technical innovation was slowing down the protective regulatory blanket that had cushioned air carriers in the US and elsewhere from the real shocks of a competitive environment began to diminish, the US government started contemplating the re-deregulation of the industry.

In summary then, the US air transport business had, by 1978, been accustomed to growing in a stable, relatively protected environment for the previous 40 years. In this scenario, not too much went drastically wrong but huge quick successes were not, shall we say, prevalent either. The positive supporting technical advancements which had caused large increases in efficiency and productivity were all but completely absorbed into the system with nothing new to follow. Therefore, just as the reliance on sounder and more innovative management practices was increasing, in order to make up for lessened impact of technical advancement, the industry was confronted with the much less comfortable prospect of real cut-throat commercial competition. Even though it may sound like the regulators had not really considered their case adequately in that perhaps the timing of re-deregulation was wrong, there is a key factor which would tend to balance the equation. This factor is the perceived

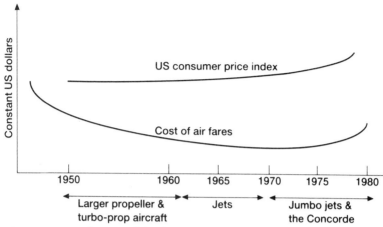

Figure 1.3 **Evolution of air fares and aviation technology since the Second World War**

maturity of the industry as a whole. It is true that by the 1970s the industry had developed into a safe, comprehensive, reliable and convenient mode of public transportation. The carriers were doing relatively well and many therefore argued that the protective regulation put in place in 1938 had done its job and it was now time to leave the industry to its own devices like any other economic sector. As we shall see, the consequences after 1978 were rather turbulent as was to be expected from an industry management group that had never really had to depend upon and cater solely for the consumer. (Figs 1.2 and 1.3)

Things in Europe developed in similar fashion with economic regulation taking hold faster than it had in the US. The major difference was, of course, that governments also set up their own carriers thereby all but eliminating scheduled carrier competition in the early years. The passing of the Second World War also served to heighten the political implications of having one's own flag carrier. At this time the US was also a step ahead in technology, thus forcing the Europeans to speed up their own development after the war. Unlike the Americans, who had many war surplus aircraft and an air transport infrastructure intact, the Europeans had to rebuild from scratch in many cases. As such the redevelopment of the system after the war made it more expensive to build and develop than in the US. All of the aforementioned conspired to make carrier reliance on government help an essential part of European carriers' development after the war. It also made the barriers to entry that much higher for the few smaller, non-government owned carriers around in the 1950s. In fact, the principles upon which European civil aviation rebuilt itself after the war can be summarized in these exerpts from a UK policy document of 1946:

a major theme running through this [document] is that governments have special interests in the development of the air transport industry and that some kind of regulation of the airlines is necessary to secure these aims of the national policy [19].

The intention of the 1946 Act was quite clearly that the operation and the development of scheduled air services should be the exclusive responsibility of the air corporations (BOAC and BEA, both UK government owned) [20].

Finally, the dichotomy between commercial and political aims was also apparent: 'governments often have substantial reasons for requiring airlines to do things which they would not do if they were acting purely as commercial undertakings [21].'

In a general sense, Europe developed as a group of state-owned flag carriers, each the favoured son of their respective government. Since few of the European nations had a significant domestic market to speak of, most (both intra-European and intercontinental) of the routes awarded were done so on the basis of restrictive bilateral agreements. Some local commuter type carriers as well as some charter (supplemental) carriers did emerge, although here again many of these were linked in some fashion to the home flag carrier. The possible exception to this would have been the UK that did have a rather large domestic market, by European standards. The Berlin airlift caused no less than 69 private airlines to form in the UK. By 1957 there were only 30 left and by 1963 this figure had dwindled to 15. This phenomenon was not duplicated elsewhere in Europe, however. An interesting facet of European aviation that was not immediately evident in the US was a strong degree of intermodal competition. After the reconstruction the rail, highway and internal waterway systems were effective competitors for transportation of goods and passengers. As a result there was more price competition in the late 1950s and 1960s between modes than in the US. This prompted the continued search for cheaper methods of air transport than the full price scheduled air seat. This among other factors conspired to create a much stronger charter airline community in Europe.

In summary then, early development of air transport management practice had explored many of the concepts and airline structures we

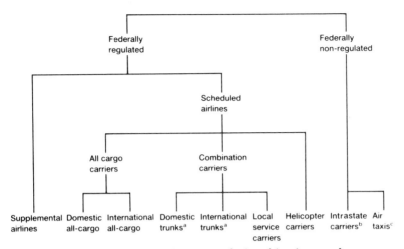

Figure 1.4 **Regulatory/Carrier type relationships in pre-deregulated USA**

know today, including the no-frills airline, the flag carrier, the low cost charter airline, market peaking, cross-subsidization, deregulation, reregulation, vertical integration (The Boeing Airplane Company owned its own airline but it eventually lost it in a merger of several carriers which eventually formed United Airlines. Such supplier/airline relationships have since been restricted although a recent deal between Boeing and United would have allowed Boeing to buy equity in United in exchange for aircraft. This deal was eventually blocked), subsidization, attempts to raise utilization by flying each aircraft for more hours per day, the frequency strategy, bankruptcy, infrastructural constraints on air transport system, intermodal competition, first class to cattle class service levels etc. Through the early years a certain cyclicality did develop. It may lead one to contemplate whether we are all just riding on a roller coaster or predictable change where the only real variable is the speed with which change occurs. In the early days of the 1920s and 1930s change was rapid because air transportation was trying to survive in the face of a consumer that did not believe air transport was a viable system for mass public transport. In order to allow the system to develop, the political powers nurtured it with regulatory protection, of one form or another, and subsidized both the infrastructure and in some cases the carriers directly. As the system developed and matured the industry experienced a veritable renaissance in technology. With this technological gain came improved efficiencies and productivity. Once these gains in technology had been absorbed into the system, the need for enhanced management skills and a greater reliance on client relations developed. It seemed natural at this point that the industry be given a chance to operate like any other industry sector. The infrastructure had developed as had the carriers, to the point where it was felt they no longer required protection from the rigours of the open market. It was normal that this re-deregulation phase be initiated in the largest domestic market in the world. In a single political entity all the rules would be set and enforced by one jurisdiction. Many of the market circumstances which prevailed in 1920–30 are once again duplicating themselves in the 1980s. We have come full circle. The US industry was unregulated back in the 1920s and 1930s but could not stand on its own two feet. Having come through a gestation period of 40-odd years, air transportation has emerged anew to return to open competition within certain domestic jurisdictions. The next two important questions are:

(1)   How long will it take the industry to be completely unregulated (in an economic context)? and

(2)   What event or series of events could conspire to firmly entrench us all on the return road to government intervention and protective regulation? In the 1930s it was the cost of conquering air travel, in the 1990s it could be the cost of developing hypersonic travel or a mass space travel system. After all, how many airlines do you know who could afford to pay $500 million or $700 million for a single new hypersonic aircraft, not to mention the entirely new infrastructure that must be developed to operate it?

2 The US marketplace

'Even in the best regulated of families accidents will occur...'

Charles Dickens

'The US air transportation market is the closest thing to legalized warfare in US business today.'

R. Crandall, American Airlines, 1986

Back in the second half of the 1970s many were questioning whether re-deregulation was the right option for the future evolution of the US air transport industry. It seems that in the late 1980s, 10 years after the big event, many Americans are still wondering whether Dickens was referring to air transport deregulation when he talked of accidents. 'Congressional support for airline deregulation has nose-dived in the four years since the Senate voted 83 to 9 and the House 363 to 8 to let the invisible hand of the market rule the airways [22].' That did not surprise John Robson, the pro-deregulation CAB Chairman during the Ford administration: 'Let's not kid ourselves,' he says, 'Fred Kahn and I had a window of about four years, when we had stable fuel prices, a growing economy, widespread discontent with government regulation, and strong White House support. I guarantee you, if congress were voting on airline deregulation today [1983], it would not pass [23].' The common feeling is that deregulation would not pass in 1987 either, despite a pro-big business Republican administration.

The US industry develops

In 1978 it seemed that the time was right. Then President Carter was reaching the mid-point of his first, and as it turned out only, term in office. This is traditionally the time when incumbent administrations begin to prepare themselves for the upcoming election two years hence. True to fashion, the Carter administration began trying to perform public-pleasing acts and air transportation deregulation was promised as a saviour for consumers of air travel. Prices would drop, new entrant carriers would improve service and offer a variety of different air travel products. Saving money for consumers was seen as especially important in 1977–8 because inflation was running at a high rate.

US consumer price index (CPI) (1975=100)

1977	1978	1979	1980
112.7	121.2	134.9	153.1

Traditionally, air carriers had raised fares at a far slower pace than inflation. However, due to large increases in the cost of fuel and significant wage increases in the late early and mid-1970s, the cost of air travel was increasing at a faster than usual pace. It is true that with the gradual slowing of technological advancement, the traditional improvements in productivity and cost savings were greatly reduced. As a result the increasing costs were not offset by a technological leap and therefore the real cost began to escalate. The Carter administration was not too keen to see consumers having to pay higher fares. A second political concern was then, as it is now, the budget deficit. Trying to trim government bureaucratic fat was just as popular a rallying cry then as today. Therefore, when it was projected that the CAB (Civil Aeronautics Board) could be abolished, thereby cutting back on government cost, it seemed as though all the necessary ingredients for political action were coming together at an opportune moment.

One of the problems was that many of the promises made by the politicians did not come to fruition, and those that did came to pass for different reasons. A senior US air official was quoted as saying, 'it is easy to vote for deregulation when its advocates promised everybody a free lunch. But now that all the goodies (lower air fares, more service) have gone to places like New York, Los Angeles, and Chicago, things look different to the guy from East Overshoe [smaller towns].' The issue of which consumers would be getting the lower fares was never quite fully explained to the travelling public. In a free market system the only markets where one has to compete on price are those where there are other competitors who are doing the same thing. In many of the smaller US markets, competition did not increase. Deregulation was a signal to some carriers that they could now abandon the less profitable smaller markets. Over 200 communities experienced reduction or loss of service. Carriers began to concentrate on the fatter markets. In these markets, price was either not affected or increased apace with inflation. These less exciting realizations did not mean that deregulation was a completely negative thing. In fact many carriers were openly disappointed with the prevailing system of regulation in the mid-1970s. While the larger US carriers did not espouse deregulation, they did seek a lessening of commercial constraint, all except United Airlines

One suspects that the larger carriers also wished to block the predicted flood of new entrant carriers that would threaten their traditional strongholds. All agreed that the system had become a little stifling:

in 1952, to compensate for poor financial results, the carriers asked the Civil Aeronautics Board's approval for a $1/ticket fare increase and removal of round-trip discounts. The fare increase was allowed but the discontinuance of the round-trip discount was not. The $1 flat rate fare increase constituted the first recognition of the principle that fare/mile should decline with distance to follow the pattern of cost/mile [24].

As a result of this action and a concerted push from the US Congress, the CAB held a General Passenger Fare Investigation (GPFI) in 1956. The general aim was to set consistent industry-wide policies for fares. The opinion of the Board was made public in 1960 but, in the interim,

the 1957–58 recession and presidential pressure caused the CAB to grant a temporary increase of 4% plus $1/ticket despite the relatively high earnings levels of the carriers in the preceding years of the decade. The carriers followed in 1958 with proposals for eliminating the round-trip discounts and free stop-overs; the family discount was also to be cut from one-half to one-third off the regular fare. The proposals were allowed by the CAB [25].

The general result of the GPFI was that a fixed rate of return was decided upon in order to aid the regulators in determining whether fare hikes, or the curtailing of discount fares, should be allowed. It was decided that large US trunk carriers would be allowed a fair rate of return of 10.5 per cent while the smaller ones would be allowed 12 per cent. In 1970 the CAB went through a similar exercise and, as was the case in the 1950s, the GPFI preceded a recession. In this case the oil crisis was the main nemesis. The main points to come out of the 1970 GPFI were:

1. In relation to fare level, the CAB found 'that the higher the fare

level in relation to cost, the more capacity carriers will offer and the lower load factors will be, the converse is also true' [26].

2. Thus the CAB set specific seating plans (number of seats abreast) and the pitch (how far apart lengthwise); this way they controlled capacity measures in order to gauge fares. Any more spacious seat arrangement than the prescribed one would require a higher fare charge. (This went against previous CAB rulings in the 1960s.)

3. Load factors (percentage of seats filled/seats offered) were set at 55 per cent for trunks and 44 per cent for locals as recommended levels. The rate of return was fixed at 12 per cent.

4. On fare structure issues, the CAB moved further towards 'a fare structure that provided a closer relationship between fares and the costs of service relating to various markets' [27].

As a result, the CAB raised short-haul fares and reduced long-haul ones. Lastly, the CAB determined that discount fares, such as family, youth and Discover America, were discriminatory. This last decision was contrary to previous CAB policy. Having looked at the type of rule-making that the CAB was involved in, it becomes clear that it had become pervasive in its interference. In addition, the reversal of policy on things like discount fares cost the carriers many millions in wasted advertising and marketing. This led to the issue of the qualification of CAB appointees to perform their jobs in a correct and competent fashion.

One salient weakness of the Civil Aeronautics Act is the incorporation in the declaration of policy of words and phrases which have been interpreted as inviting regulators to mix promotional aims with the more basic objectives of economic regulation [28].

A prime factor in what many feel has been misdirected regulation has been a high incidence of Board members seemingly ill-equipped by either experience or training to deal with industry problems [29].

In fact the vagueness of the Act in some areas combined with varying levels of competence among appointees led the CAB to become a stifling influence on the industry.

For those airlines lucky enough to be allowed into the certificated industry, the CAB initially seemed more of a protection than a control. Individual attention to airline problems allowed the CAB to adjust subsidies and elevate fares according to need, with little regard for efficiency. Standardization, however, increasingly curbed managerial freedom as individual company strategies inevitably had to be brought into line with the flock [30].

Service – including capacity – remained about the only sector for managerial action. This too was eventually brought under control through the DPFI, with the prospect of even more stringent controls in the future. For airline managements, this progression displayed a steady erosion of managerial freedom to the point that routes, capacities, and fares were increasingly fixed [31].

Even the various methods of carrier growth, including mergers or acquisitions, were all controlled by the CAB. Virtually all the major levers of control that were exercisable by management had been usurped by the CAB.

The industry was spawning a generation of marketers whose most critical decisions could have been what colour the carpets and seats should be on the aircraft, or a general management group who spent their time wondering how they should convince the CAB that they wanted to grow. Lobbying the CAB became more important than what the customer may have wanted. Air transportation had gone from a wild man's method of transport, to a business, to its seemingly final incarnation as a public utility.

For many, the situation seemed ripe for freer competition or, at least, less pervasive regulation ...On the other hand, for many airlines, the prospect of deregulation was filled with uncertainties, not the least of which being the uncertainty about their abilities to manage in a very different environment [32].

It is important to note that the carriers had been gradually programmed to assume less and less responsibility for their fates. Now with the spectre of deregulation on the horizon it seemed that they would be jolted back to reality without any period of adjustment. How well prepared would these managers be? Despite this critical issue, the support for re-deregulation grew, based in practical terms on three forerunners: the intrastate markets in California and Texas, the complete deregulation of the all-cargo carrier several years earlier, and the deregulation of commuter services.

In California, Pacific Southwest Airlines and its intrastate contemporaries indulged in far freer competition. Product and price were allowed to fluctuate to a greater degree, although not completely. In Texas, Southwest Airlines fought with Braniff and Texas International for market share on intra-Texas markets. By using high frequency, low operating costs (wages etc.), standardized fleet and heavy promotion, Southwest was able to establish itself while its competition had trouble meeting its price due to their higher cost structures. In addition, Southwest used a ploy of presenting itself as the underdog carrier that should be supported because it was

American and to support free enterprise. This latter strategy met with approval in the heavily entrepreneurial state of Texas.

Cargo deregulation caused a consolidation among the bigger players such as Flying Tigers and Seabord World but also allowed the then fledgling Federal Express to go from marginal size in 1975 to the most profitable carrier in the US, bar none, in 1982. Freight forwarders and ground-based carriers such as Emery, UPS, Purolator and Burlington Northern all got involved in air cargo. As a result, the variety of services (products) offered increased greatly. In addition, the rates came down as competition increased.

The rapid increase in commuter carrier activity, characterized by increased frequency on smaller routes with smaller more flexible aircraft and an increase in discount fare products in some markets, was also seen as the beginning of liberalization of the commuter sector. Armed with these generally successful precedents, the so-called 'father of re-deregulation', Dr A Kahn, set about changing the face of passenger air travel in the US when he became CAB chairman in June 1977.

I didn't come into this job with a grand strategy. But I did come in with a strong sense of the imperfections of regulation, a healthy respect for the efficiency of markets and a predilection in favour of relying on the latter wherever effective competition appears favourable. That does not mean I am a true believer. I am well aware of the imperfections, to maintain competition, to correct market failures and to regulate 'natural monopolies'. But wherever competition seems feasible, my disposition is to put my trust in it much the same way as I do in democracy–as a manifestly inefficient system that is better than any of the alternatives [33].

This type of philosophical outlook is illustrated by a story told by Kahn:

...the incident occurred on a rainy day in Washington, when a large number of people were waiting at a bus stop on their way home from work, only to be passed time and again by full busses. An empty bus came lumbering down the opposite side of the street. The driver pulled over to the curb, opened his window and asked the very wet people across the street how long they had been waiting. Upon hearing their tale of woe, he said 'wait just a minute,' drove ahead to the next traffic circle and within a few seconds returned to pick them up and take them home. That driver could never have been regulated by the CAB [34].

Reflecting upon Kahn's intent, we note that a large change was coming, one that would force the carriers in the system to completely re-adapt their management methods and thinking. One thing that many forget to contemplate is that in returning the US industry to the unregulated state which had characterized it in the late 1920s and early 1930s, the CAB was re-installing the economic cycle as a major governing factor in the industry's future activities. It is fair to say that in the period from 1938–1978 the CAB had cushioned the airlines from the excessive ups and downs that most other industries had to face. As a result the level and consistency of consumer benefit would be conditioned by the carriers' own ability to survive the peaks and troughs of the economy. Despite all the brilliant rhetoric extolling the virtues of deregulation, the fact remained that the system had inadequately prepared incumbent airline management groups for what lay ahead. Some argue that a more phased in approach to deregulation would have helped achieve this goal, but the limited time for removing regulation was such that the political powers did not wish to prolong the deregulatory process of the industry. Therefore it was logical to assume that the first months of deregulation would be characterized by air carriers learning to live in open competition and making several mistakes along the way.

The post-1978 deregulation period

There can be no doubt that the 1978 Airline Deregulation Act opened the door to drastic change in the US domestic industry. It was change that seemed drastic for the carriers who had been trained in regulated airline management. There had been relatively little real excitement in the preceding years. There had been Delta's purchase of the old Northeast Airlines and the takeover of the Mohawk Airlines by the then Allegheny Airlines (see Fig. 2.5). These particular transactions were seen as saving actions for the two absorbed carriers and sensible network consolidations for the surviving carriers. As noted in Table 2.1, there were many carriers that were in at the start of deregulation that have since vanished.

The market was then populated by a series of relatively stable carriers. Each stayed more or less in their territories and new route access, fares and capacity were strictly regulated so the scope for significant change was also limited. All of that was to change, however. In addition to the above carrier categories, we note that commuters and charter (supplemental) airlines had remained relatively stable in composition and scope of activity. If any group had been the innovators it would have been the charter carriers who had

Table 2.1 Pre-deregulation carriers

Trunk carriers	Local service	All-cargo
American	Aloho	Airlift International
Braniff	Air New England	Flying Tiger Line
Continental	Allegheny (US Air)	Seabord World
Delta	Frontier	Federal Express–1975
Eastern	Hughes Airwest	
National	North Central	
Northwest	Ozark	
Pan American	Piedmont	
Trans World	Southern	
United	Texas International	
Western	Pacific Southwest	
	Southwest	
	Wien Air	
	Hawaiian Airlines	
	(plus others)	

enjoyed more regulatory freedom to exit and enter markets and charge differentiated fares when compared to the freedoms allowed the scheduled carriers. The supplementals were in fact the only group of carriers that could consider that they offered a differentiated and segmented product to the air travel buying public. Unfortunately deregulation would spell a practical end to the supplemental type carriers because most of the new entrants sought to enter the same low-cost, low-service type of product category thus removing the only original product feature that the supplementals had possessed up until then.

Having briefly introduced the curious and seemingly unique circumstances under which deregulation had come about, let us now focus in on the actual results. At the outset it is probably fair to say that very few airline managers who had been around in the pre-1938 unregulated period in air transportation were still around and in positions of authority in 1978. Such being the case, it follows that the collective US industry management group had had little if any management experience in a pure unregulated competitive environment. Apart from the knowledge of the early (pre-1938) history of air transport management techniques, many managers were on their own. These managers were getting ready, unknown to some of them, to blaze new trails, only this time the new trails would not be technically or airmanship-based but management skills-based. This was a radical departure for many. It was, however, a welcome opportunity to attempt market and industry domination for others.

Early strategies—surpassing the traditional 'golden rules'

A set of so-called 'golden rules' were evolved towards which airline managers had developed a blind faith. The longer the distance flown, the better the return on investment and the more efficient the operation; a hub, any hub, was the best method to build up one's network; operating in high-volume markets was always preferable to low-density markets; were a couple of adages that seemed to abound, among others.

Overnight, these and other previously held wise truths were not only challenged but many exceptions to these so-called golden rules became apparent. Many is the time that the story is told of the line-up outside the ex-regulators office in Washington the morning after deregulation was passed, every carrier fighting to get in first to ask for more route rights. The original version of Braniff, among others, asking for hundreds more route authorities. Once having obtained these route authorities, the rule seemed to be that the best and fastest way to acquire market share in new market city pairs was, of course, to lower the fares. The regulators were dancing with glee at the prospect of cheaper fares for all consumers, as they had promised prior to the passing of the new Airline Deregulation Act. The question was, lower fares at what price?

United was obviously a firm early believer in the golden rules. They began a strategy that would see them drop out of many smaller markets and concentrate on the key transcontinental ones. After all, it had always been true that the longer the route the more efficient the operation. This was based on the simple truth that the most expensive parts of a flight were the takeoff and landing. Therefore, it stood to reason that the more distance between takeoff and landing (time at cruise altitude and configuration) the better and less expensive the operation. United had, like many other carriers, developed a network over many years that included many different sized markets. United's fleet, then the largest in the free world, was composed of several different sizes of airplane. The problem was that some of its smaller markets were a little too small for their smallest jet (the Boeing 737) and therefore these operations were assessed as inefficient. In the regulated environment, the tendency had been for United to retain these markets in an attempt to grow them to acceptable levels. A prime reason why this made sense was because new domestic US growth opportunities were rather limited. Now, however, the deregulated US domestic market presented United with a plethora of seemingly viable commercial opportunities. It seemed that the rational thing to do was to abandon these smaller markets and concentrate on the bigger medium- and long-haul markets. United could streamline the number of types in its fleet and replace marginal short-haul routes with better ones.

This is exactly what United began doing. They abandoned many smaller routes and initiated a reduction in the size of their smallest fleet type (B-737). They also increased their presence in the premium long-haul markets. It all made sense: a large carrier prior to deregulation, United thought it could become dominant in many larger markets and improve its overall viability. A relatively short period afterwards, United reversed its strategy. Why? Some of the key reasons revolve around the fact that United had exercised what would have been considered good decision-making in a regulated environment but one which failed to recognize the new realities.

First of all, the long-haul markets became less desirable for two reasons. The first was that virtually every carrier thought that the long-haul routes were best and therefore a large increase in competition occurred in these markets. In fact, by 1982 none of the airlines flying the transcontinental routes was making as much as a 1 per cent return on sales. The large influx of new competition brought with it the inevitable corollary of price wars. Price reductions were necessary because the supply of seats quickly began to exceed demand. Because of this, the yield on these routes dropped drastically, a 50 per cent drop in fares on some sectors within months of deregulation. Carriers who had previously been considered supplementals, such as World, began making the New York–Los Angeles route the most price-competitive in the world. World brought with it its low price heritage which did nothing to improve the yield of its trunk carrier competitors. Because of its higher cost structure and restrictive labour work rules, United had more trouble competing on price. A second major unforeseen consequence of United's withdrawal from small markets was the attendant drop in feed traffic at its hubs. It may have been assumed that consumer loyalty that had been traditionally attached to United would simply stay with it. Unfortunately, consumer loyalty in many smaller centres went to the carriers that could get them all the way to their final destination. The concept of air hubs had already evolved into the most efficient operational network structure around. Hubs had been more difficult to develop in regulated times simply because additional market access, that may have been required to enhance the size and market catchment area of the hub, were not easy to obtain in the CAB era. In the new deregulated era, any carrier could fly any new routes it wished to, so hub building was greatly facilitated.

United soon realized this and began going back into smaller markets and re-acquiring more smaller jets in order to enhance operations into lower density markets. In contrast to United, Delta used the reverse strategy and concentrated on shorter haul routes and the building up of its super-hub in Atlanta (see Table 2.2).

Table 2.2   Distribution of stage lengths (domestic, 1981)

Stage length (miles)	% of flights	
	Delta	United
Less than 400	66	14
400 – 799	21	32
800 – 1199	10	24
1200 – 1599	10	24
1600 and over	3	9

Source: Lockheed.

Note that Delta had 87 per cent of all its domestic flights flying distances of less than 800 miles whereas United had 53 per cent of its total domestic frequencies flying 800 miles or more. This was one of the key factors which resulted in the following operating statistics for the two carriers for the 1981 year:

	Passengers	Departures	Net profit (loss)
United	28 690 000	337 492	$(104 892 937)
Delta	34 777 000	517 477	$ 91 640 000

While it would be misleading to say that Delta's network was entirely responsible for the difference, it is safe to assume that it had a definite impact on the outcome. Certainly Delta's network development activities, characterized by their direct hub enhancement strategy, would appear to have been better than United's hub dismantling followed by hub reconstruction strategy. In fact the whole issue of how to go about developing an optimal route structure was an early learning ground for many carriers. At first sight, it would seem that air hubs were contrary to the concept of optimized customer service. It would be difficult to convince a traveller that it was better to fly one-stop than non-stop.

It is also true, however, that operating through a hub where all of the outlying points are roughly equidistant from the focal point is the most efficient way to fly aeroplanes. In an era of deregulation, however, it was customer satisfaction that was to have taken precedence, or was it? It soon became evident that the hub could also enhance service to the consumer by allowing economic operation of more flights between smaller or medium-sized centres and the hub. While the use of non-stop flights was preferable, the number in any market was controlled by the market size of that city pair (e.g. New York–Los Angeles). The frequency of service in a hub connector market was contingent on how much traffic was flowing between the point of origin and all the other points connected through the hub. Therefore, in the case of a hub such as Delta's at Atlanta, with 192 departures a day (1981) that were coordinated to come and go in hub complexes (connection banks), the frequency between many points and Atlanta was much greater than could have been justified by a simple point to point non-stop frequency. This meant that one non-stop/day in any given market could be complemented by two or three one-stop flights via the hub airport. This was amenable to consumer preferences which listed frequency of service as high a priority as non-stop service in many cases. This co-mingling of traffic was therefore helpful to the airlines who operated more efficiently in a hub configuration, as well as to the consumer who got more choice of frequency. In fact, hub type operations became the so-called 'state of the art' configuration for network design. So much so that carriers began to concentrate on ways to improve hubs and their attractiveness to air travellers.

Evolution of the hubs

Piedmont Airlines had proven itself to be a competent smaller regional carrier that had served a part of the country neglected by many other carriers, namely the mid-Atlantic seaboard states. In the late 1970s and early 1980s, however, it grew at an astounding rate. As with many other carriers, Piedmont took advantage of free market access but they did not attempt to grow through acquisition of another major carrier, nor did they spend much energy on greatly expanding the geographic area that they served. Instead they concentrated on perfecting their operations in many of their familiar territories. As the first serious and concerted proponent of the perfected or second generation hub concept, Piedmont was able to attack the market with a new variation on the existing hub strategy. Piedmont became very competitive with the trunks such as Delta and

Eastern because they went beyond the simple fact of having a hub to having one of higher quality than the others. In practical terms, this meant less airport congestion which meant better on-time performance, newer facilities that were more pleasant to wait in, and the same large network of available connecting points as at the big hubs. Piedmont decided that Charlotte, NC was the point on which it would centre its operations. It got good mileage out of the fact that its main competitor, Delta, was encumbered by the delay-causing Atlanta hub that had grown very quickly over the last 24 months. Connect at a better hub, for a lower fare, was the message consumers got. It seems to have worked very well and Piedmont has managed to install itself as a major conduit for north–south traffic on the eastern seabord. See Tables 2.3 and 2.4.

Table 2.3   1981 growth in market share

US industry Rank	Carrier	Revenue passenger miles (%)	Market share (%)
1	Piedmont	+36.9	+41.1
2	Frontier	+17.8	+21.9
4	Republic	+ 7.9	+11.3
9	Delta	− 4.1	− 1.1
13	United	− 9.4	− 6.5

Table 2.4   Operating profit and operating margin for traditional carriers, 1981 (first 9 months)

Rank	Carrier	Op. profit (ooo)	Op. margin (%)
1	Piedmont	$41.5	10.2
2	Frontier	$41.9	9.6
4	US Air	$41.7	5.1
6	Delta	$84.4	3.1
12	United	−$25.5	−0.7

As Piedmont itself says,

Traditionally we had operated into New York and Chicago. Now when deregulation came along, all those super franchises [routes], the airlines had for so long and that were reportedly worth millions of dollars were now open for the taking...and we chose not to get into it and we certainly have no intention of getting into it...instead we chose a very different philosophy which was really two pronged. First, was a philosophy of bypassing regular route junction points. ...The second prong to our philosophy, of course, has been a matter of feeding ourselves, the so-called hub and spoke concept [35].

The added beauty of the Piedmont strategy was that they spread their risk by building up hubs at not only Charlotte but Dayton and Baltimore as well. By serving Baltimore/Washington airport (BWI), Piedmont was clearly accessing the Washington market without having to build a major presence at a slot-restricted airport (Washington National). The fact that Piedmont had several hubs meant that by definition they were less vulnerable than, say, Delta that at the time had only one real hub. Piedmont and US Air had similar feed and market penetration and selection strategies. They stayed in the smaller medium-sized markets where the levels of competition were lower, yields higher and the chance to build up regional loyalties better due to the fact that these carriers took you all the way to your final destination. A sub-strategy was the liberal use of commuter carriers to feed traffic to smaller jet-prone markets and build up grass-roots level feed. There was good money to be made in connecting medium-sized centres to each other, smaller centres to each other and medium and smaller centres to the big ones. Both Piedmont and US Air seem to have been adept at capitalizing on these circumstances. As the 1980s progressed, it can be noted that multi-hub operations began to spring up everywhere. Delta, American, Continental and others all got involved in multi-hub operations which served to spread risk and allow a multi-pronged attack against competitors. Looking at what used to be a winning strategy for Piedmont in the early 1980s, one must re-evaluate how long it will work. United has set up a competing Washington area hub at Dulles (100 flights/day by 1988). Delta has picked Cincinnati as its Ohio hub while Continental is trying to turn Cleveland into its Ohio hub, in addition to Piedmont's Dayton hub. Raleigh-Durham has welcomed an American Airlines hub, which by 1989 will have 280 daily flights by AA and AA Eagle commuters, while Memphis is another American Airlines hub.

These hubs are in addition to the well-known ones such as United's Chicago Continental's and United's competing Denver hubs, TWA's St Louis and Delta's Salt Lake City (ex-Western) and Atlanta (see Table 2.5). The issue for Piedmont will be how to maintain leadership in the hubs war. Their own hubs at Charlotte, Baltimore and Dayton are becoming busy and over time could be congested and reminiscent of the Atlanta type centres they were designed to replace. When their existing hubs become too congested, where will they establish their next hub ? Will there be any cities with a population over 100 left?

Table 2.5 Major US city population versus air activity comparison, 1984

US city	Rank	Population (millions)	Rank	Air traffic (millions of passengers per year)
New York	1	18.03	3	18.58
Los Angeles	2	12.49	4	17.37
Chicago	3	8.55	1	18.95
Philadelphia	4	7.37	18	3.98
San Francisco	5	6.07	6	11.65
Boston	6	5.78	10	8.04
Detroit	7	5.10	16	4.89
Washington	8	4.11	11	7.89
Houston	9	4.10	9	8.50
Cleveland	10	3.89	21	2.63
Miami	11	3.83	8	9.94
Dallas/Ft.W.	12	3.74	5	15.68
St Louis	13	3.53	12	7.82
Pittsburgh	14	3.36	14	5.54
Hartford	15	3.22	29	1.42
Minneapolis	16	3.20	13	5.78
Seattle	17	3.08	15	4.96
Atlanta	18	3.07	2	18.65
Tampa	19	3.05	19	3.83
Memphis	20	2.68	24	2.36
Baltimore	21	2.53	25	2.30
Phoenix	22	2.23	17	4.80
Denver	23	2.17	7	11.40
Portland	24	2.16	26	2.07
New Orleans	25	2.14	22	2.87
San Diego	26	2.14	20	3.14

Source: Lloyd's Aviation Economist

Many are projecting a return to more point-to-point non-stop services. One of the reasons for this suggestion involves the varied behaviour of the consumer. In healthy economic times when fares and yields go up, will passengers demand better schedule integrity and superior hub performance and fewer stops on the way to wherever they are going? While some of these factors may conspire to increase the number of non-stops, few would say that hubs will disappear. In fact additional airports, or capacity within existing infrastructures at major airports, should grow over the next 5–10 years with new airports at such places as Denver. It is interesting to observe that the advent of deregulation has given carriers the chance to completely wean themselves away from linear schedules. Carriers can then progress through the simple hub and spoke and beyond to second-generation (perfected) to multiple combinations of large, medium and mini-hubs all operated by the same carrier.

Strategic snapshot: USAir/Piedmont

(*Source: The Avmark Aviation Economist May 1987*)

A marriage made in airline heaven or not?

In March this year (1987) the Piedmont board of directors accepted a $1.59bn proposal from USAir and, although the implications of the merger were investigated by the Department of Transportation, they were eventually approved. This will be an unusual merger as the two airlines are successful (they have both just announced record traffic and profit figures for the first quarter 1987) and share a similar pedigree, having developed from local service carriers. While the merger looks genuinely synergistic, the new combine will face a new set of challengers and problems.

Pre-merger similarities

The most remarkable similarity between Piedmont and USAir is their profitability. Their parent companies, Piedmont Aviation, Inc. and USAir Group Inc., have returned net profit figures every year since the introduction of US deregulation. In 1986, Piedmont achieved an operating profit of $164.4m and a net profit of $72.4m on revenues of $1.87bn; USAir made an operating profit of $169.4m and a net profit of $98.4m on revenues of $1.84bn.

In producing these results, Piedmont and USAir have used similar strategic approaches, and the management in both companies has been characterized by stability and relative longevity.

Piedmont's chairman and chief executive officer, William R Howard, has been at the airline since 1978. Edwin Colodny, USAir's chairman and chief executive officer since 1975, joined Allegheny Airlines (USAir's former name) back in 1957.

Both carriers were early believers in the benefits of commuter feed and have recently been consolidating their secondary networks. In 1986 Piedmont bought the Syracuse-, New York, based Empire Airlines and integrated its operations into its own, so ensuring strong feed from the New England and southern Canada areas. In 1986, Jetstream International became a wholly-owned subsidiary of Piedmont, providing commuter traffic to the Dayton, Ohio, hub. Piedmont has also set up an extensive intra-Florida commuter network, under the brand name 'Piedmont Shuttle', operated by the Piedmont Regional Airline, formerly Henson Aviation. This carrier is now flying more than a hundred daily departures and is in the process of expanding both within Florida and in North and South Carolina. Piedmont also had (1987) marketing agreements with two independent commuter airlines—CCAir which provided feed to the Charlotte, North Carolina, hub and Brockway Air which operates mainly in upstate New York.

USAir has relied on the long-established Allegheny Commuter system, the seven members of which carried some 2m passengers in 1985, 45 per cent of them connecting to or from USAir flights. In 1985 and 1986 USAir acquired the two largest Allegheny commuters, Pennsylvania Airlines and Suburban Airlines, both of which have been expanding their feed systems at the Philadelphia hub.

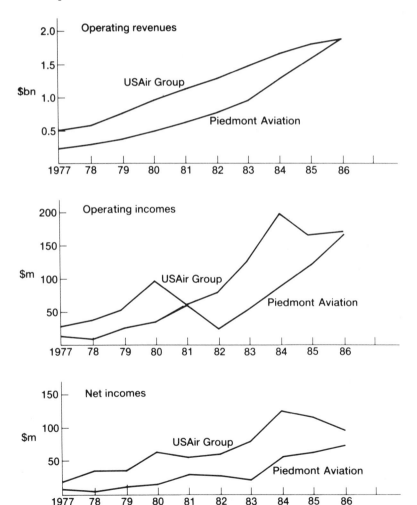

In late 1986 USAir announced an agreement to purchase California-based Pacific Southwest Airlines (PSA), the most important carrier in the Los Angeles–San Francisco market. In mid-May (1987) approval was given for the $400m takeover.

The Piedmont Shuttle operation, the ex-Empire intra-New England network and the PSA Californian service employ exclusively jet aircraft, F28s or BAe 146. As many business travellers complain about the uncomfortable feeling of flying in smaller turboprop aircraft on secondary routes, using jets seems to be an effective way of segmenting their more important commuter routes from their competitors'.

Both carriers developed the second-generation hub concept. They recognized that simply having a hub was not enough and instead sought to develop hubs which offered better on-time performance potential, more pleasant and less crowded facilities for passengers, and superior connections.

Accordingly, Piedmont adopted a strategy of siphoning Atlanta traffic through its Charlotte hub and Washington National traffic through its Baltimore/Washington hub. It focused on Dayton as a hub in the immediate post-deregulation period when many major carriers deserted this city. Concentrating on local business travel, the airline was able to operate profitably and take advantage of the city's willingness to finance expansion of the airport.

Like Piedmont, USAir has concentrated on unglamourous routes, developing its main pre-deregulation hub at Pittsburg. Although Pittsburg's image in the early '80s was not too attractive—it was the centre of the severely depressed US steel industry—USAir was able to offer good amenities at the airport. And, Pittsburg's standing as both a business centre and as a place to live has risen dramatically in recent years; in 1985 it emerged as top city in a listing of socio-economic indicators.

In keeping with their hub strategies, both carriers have adopted similar competitive tactics. Neither has tried to take on any of the larger carriers at their own hubs and have avoided trying to compete head-to-head with other

FIRST QUARTER RESULTS ($ million)		
Piedmont	1st quarter 1987	1st quarter 1986
Operating revenues	460.88	404.14
Operating costs	449.83	405.23
Operating Profit (loss)	11.06	(1.09)
Net profit	5.66	(6.92)
USAir		
Operating revenues	449.87	400.46
Operating costs	421.77	414.09
Operating Profit (loss)	28.09	13.63
Net profit	18.90	(8.07)

Majors. In many sectors Piedmont and USAir have near-monopoly positions and so have found it relatively easy to set the pace on product and price.

The high yields obtained in these markets have enabled them to withstand the competitive pressures on the few routes where there is a significant overlap with a strong competitor. In 1986, Piedmont's yield was 15.2 cents per PPM and USAir's 14.8 cents per RPM, compared with a US industry average of 10.8 cents. However, partly as a consequence of having developed from local service bases, neither carrier has been strong in the computer reservations area and they have had to rely on the dominant systems to sell their flights.

Before Piedmont's recent acquisition of Charlotte-London rights, neither carrier had been interested in international routes although both had international traffic feed agreements, Piedmont with TWA and USAir with Pan Am. But, neither carriers' in-flight products have been particularly good compared to international standards. Piedmont has had considerable lead over USAir in this field, recently adding first class to all its flights, a move that USAir did not agree to until mid-1988

Low-cost new-entrant carriers caused both Piedmont and USAir some problems in the early phase of deregulation as neither carrier placed great emphasis on operating cost reductions and USAir's labour costs are still among the highest in the US industry. In 1986, Piedmont's and USAir's unit costs were 8.6 cents per ASM and 8.9 cents per ASM respectively, compared with an industry average of 7.4 cents.

Both airlines have been active in ordering new aircraft, Piedmont more than USAir. Piedmont was a launch customer for the 737-400, placing orders for 25 aircraft last June, and, at almost the same time, booking six 767-200 Extended Range twinjets. The company's commitments for these aircraft, plus 27 737-300s, 14 BAe Jetstreams and 12 DeHavilland Dash-8s, totalled $1.84bn at the end of 1986. USAir's purchase agreements at the end of 1986 were for 25 737-300s and 20 Fokker 100s at a total cost of about $870m.

USAir's and Piedmont's financial bases have been strengthened over recent years, and these investments should not produce too much strain. USAir's debt/equity ratio at the end of 1986 was 0.43:1 (or 30%/70%) on a capitalisation of $1.51bn while Piedmont's was 0.38:1 (or 29%/71%) on a capitalisation of $1.10bn. At USAir, cash flow (net income plus depreciation) was $191m in 1986 compared with interest expenses of $31m; at Piedmont cash flow was $189m and interest expenses $50m.

The post-merger period

The merging of USAir and Piedmont (AL/PI) will certainly create a whole that is stronger than the sum of the parts. A good network fit will enable the new AL/PI to draw significant feed from strong intra-zone carriers in New England, Florida and California. Also, these three feeder networks will generate important revenues simply from local traffic.

The Northeast is experiencing a revival as service industries replace the previously dominant heavy manufacturing companies; Florida state has been among the US' economic growth leaders; and California has more air travel within its borders than most countries. In sum, AL/PI will benefit from dominant feed networks in the US' most important economic growth regions.

The new network also gives the AL/PI combination a dominant position among secondary hub operations, although the competition is catching up quickly. With Pittsburg, Charlotte, Baltimore, Dayton and Philadelphia, the new airline will be able to mount a strong presence on the Mid-Atlantic seaboard and in the mid-US zone.

A powerful north-south network should be the result of the merger, but AL/PI will have rather weak connections on east-west routes, with low frequencies from a limited number of points. Piedmont and USAir management might worry about the experience of the former Republic Airlines which was formed through a merger of three relatively strong regional airlines (North Central, Hughes Airwest and Southern), but had considerable difficulties in developing strong links between the three networks. Such a problem is, however, less likely in the AL/PI case as their major hubs are closer to one another.

While the AL/PI merger should generate efficiencies in the management ranks and create the potential for overhead cost savings, it will also cause some friction between the various unions involved.

Although USAir in late 1985 introduced a two-tier pay scale which narrows but never actually closes wage differentials between existing employees and new hires over a five year period, after which the contract is due for renegotiation, average annual compensation for USAir (including PSA) was $46,800 in the third quarter of last year, just under the Pan Am figure. At Piedmont, by contrast, average annual compensation was $33,100, just under the figure for Texas Air Corp. employees. Piedmont's (and PSA's) labour policies have also included greater degrees of profit-sharing, employee participation and job flexibility than USAir's. These differences could result in

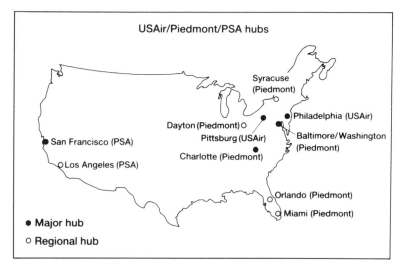

USAir/Piedmont/PSA hubs

Syracuse (Piedmont)

Philadelphia (USAir)

Dayton (Piedmont)

Pittsburg (USAir)

Baltimore/Washington (Piedmont)

San Francisco (PSA)

Charlotte (Piedmont)

Los Angeles (PSA)

Orlando (Piedmont)

Miami (Piedmont)

● Major hub
○ Regional hub

contentious negotiations at a time when the combine could come under increased pressure on pricing.

PIEDMONT'S AND USAIR'S FLEETS

	In operation		On order		Options	
	Piedmont	USAir	Piedmont	USAir	Piedmont	USAir
767-ER	—	—	6	—	6	—
727-200	34	13	—	—	—	—
737-400	—	—	25	—	30	—
737-300	19	23	28	25	10	—
737-200	62	23	—	—	—	—
DC-9-30	70	—	—	—	—	—
BAe 1-11	20	—	—	—	—	—
Fokker 100	—	—	—	20	—	20
F28	45	—	—	—	—	—

Notes: As at Dec. 31, 1986. PSA's fleet (including orders) comprises 21 BAe 146s, 4 DC-9-30s and 27 MD-80s.

With a jet fleet of over 400 the AL/PI grouping will rank sixth in the US in terms of seat capacity, but in the combined fleet there are duplications of aircraft type, making some rationalization probable. The DC-9-30 fleet may be replaced and any significant increase in the fuel price could cause the sale of the 727-200s.

As mentioned above, the AL/PI presence in computer reservations systems was minimal until USAir purchased a share in a major US CRS system which should resolve this issue. With route network consolidation, fleet re-equipment, international expansion and possible labour cost problems, it was unlikely that AL/PI would have been able to devote the resources necessary to build up its own in-house computerized system.

The longer term

International expansion is an important issue for the AL/PI grouping. Piedmont was a very late entrant into the transatlantic market – its daily 767-200ER Charlotte to London which started on June 15, 1987 – and the question now is whether this represents a one-off venture or the beginning of a concerted push overseas.

If AL/PI does decide to go for the international market, the fastest way of achieving its objective, given the airlines' relatively strong financial positions, would be to purchase TWA or Pan Am. But Ed Colodny recently turned down Carl Icahn's proposal that if TWA was not allowed to buy USAir, then USAir should buy TWA. A more likely outcome might be for AL/PI to consolidate and develop the already existing commercial alliances with TWA and/or Pan Am—or to form links with a foreign carrier.

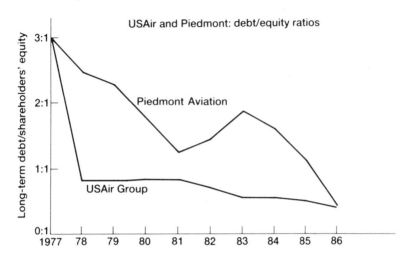

USAir and Piedmont: debt/equity ratios

PIEDMONT AND USAIR:
BREAKDOWN OF 1986 OPERATING COSTS

	Piedmont	USAir
Personnel	33.5%	41.3%
Fuel	13.7%	14.3%
Landing fees, etc.	7.1%	5.0%
Maintenance and repairs	6.2%	4.3%
Depreciation & amortization	6.9%	5.6%
Commissions	7.0%	7.5%
Others	25.6%	22.0%
Total	100.0%	100.0%
Total ($million)	1.70	1.67

If KLM wins its rights to extend foreign carrier designators, it will achieve much greater access to the US domestic market and the AL/PI combine could fit well into this expansion strategy.

As almost purely domestic carriers, the AL/PI combine is very exposed to the US economic cycle, and some pessimistic forecasters claim that the economy now shows signs of downturn. Cost control will become critical for the new grouping in such circumstances. Major investment programmes may mean a reduction in the profit-sharing plans that Piedmont and PSA employees have become used to, bringing a new set of union pressures.

Finally, the AL/PI strategy of developing second-generation, high quality hubs will also come under pressure. As Piedmont moves to 280-plus daily departures at Baltimore/Washington and 370-plus at Charlotte, the imminent danger is that conditions at these airports will come to resemble those which the hubs were originally designed to avoid. There are no easy solutions to this emerging problem.

Opening up new second-generation hubs is difficult as the other Majors are taking up most of the available candidates – American at Raleigh-Durham, and Delta at Cincinnati, for example, This trend will have two effects on the AL/PI combine. First, it brings the new airline into much closer head-to-head competition with the other Majors and, second, it will remove some of AL/PI's potential for growth.

Another solution would be to keep expanding and improving facilities at existing hubs to keep ahead of traffic growth. Regional hubs such as Syracuse (New York) and Orlando (Florida) could be made into major hubs, as could developmental points like Greensboro (North Carolina).

Whatever choices the new AL/PI group makes, it is certain that it will be a major force to be reckoned with in the future.

Big is beautiful?

Another popular assumption in the early days of deregulation was that big was beautiful or size for the sake of size. The name Braniff quickly comes to mind when thinking of carriers who tried to grow faster than their structure allowed them to. The enormous cost and structural (management, technical, etc) stress of rapid growth, in times of declining yields, was one of the key downfalls of Braniff. Other examples of this seemingly ill-fated strategy included the early attempts at merger. The methods for massive growth in the late 1970s and early 1980s were either internally generated growth or growth through acquisition and mergers. While carriers such as American chose to grow through internal means, Pan Am (who bought National) and North Central (merged with Southern and Hughes Airwest) airlines decided to try the mergers and acquisitions route (see Fig. 2.5).

It is commonly agreed that these two mergers were detrimental to the carriers involved. Many analysts of the day were saying that the merger and acquisitions strategy was simply a bad strategy. While the two examples may have given these analysts ample cause to question the effectiveness of mergers, we have since seen that the late 1980s is proving a more fertile period for this type of growth. Back in the early stages of deregulation, Pan Am attempted to fix many of the problems they felt they had by acquiring National Airlines. After all, National had been doing fairly well and its Miami base was proving an increasingly vibrant market from which to operate. Additionally, the National route structure had something Pan Am desperately wanted, a relatively strong domestic route base. National's costs were lower than Pan Am's and this was thought to be a potentially helpful feature for Pan Am. National had also developed some transatlantic routes from Miami to various points in Europe and Pan Am felt that this would help consolidate its dominant Atlantic position. In addition, the level of pre-flight, in-flight and post flight service was better perceived than that of Pan Am in many markets. All in all it looked like a good marriage. Almost steadily since the purchase of National, however, Pan Am has been going downhill. Why? First, it is a commonly accepted rule of efficiency that the number of different aircraft types in a given carrier's fleet should be limited. This reduces pilot training costs, maintenance training costs, the cost of spare parts inventories and the overall complexity of the operation. In buying National, Pan Am found itself with all three widebody fleet types (747, L-1011 and DC-10) in their fleet.

The perceived cost advantage of National was quickly lost when the union seniority list integration exercise began. So bitter were these negotiations that it took many months to partially complete the task which has had lingering morale implications to this day. The eventual outcome was that National came up to Pan Am's rate as opposed to the reverse. Many of the domestic routes of the previous National network were in fact overlapping those of Pan Am, reducing the actual benefit of network integration. Finally, the sheer cost of financing the takeover was almost too much for Pan Am to bear. A combination of the operating losses that the merger generated and the actual debt load necessitated by the acquisition, put Pan Am in a hole from which it has yet to extricate itself. A series of sell-offs (including aircraft, a hotel chain, the Pan Am building in New York and Pan Am's valuable Pacific route network) has been consummated in order to help avoid bankruptcy. Recently the Pan Am board of directors authorized sales of all of Pan Am's (airlines) assets.

Similarly, the merger of Southern and North Central, later joined by Hughes Airwest, seemed a stroke of genius at the outset. The three carriers had strong regional bases from which to operate. North Central at Minneapolis, Southern at Atlanta and Hughes Airwest in the western part of the US made it seem like an ideal non-overlapping joint network. All three operated similar sized, mostly DC-9, aircraft fleets, although various prop aircraft were also part of the combined fleet. Things looked good until the merger of union seniority lists began generating similar problems to those experienced by Pan Am. Although the three carriers were segregated to various distinct portions of the US domestic market, the integration of the route network was difficult. Whose marginal routes got the funding to develop? North Central's, Southern's or Hughes Airwest's? Was there a more important geographic area of the airline? Even though North Central, now Republic, was the surviving carrier, the early period was difficult because the ex-management groups of all three airlines were trying to become one. The adoption of the new single Republic image helped but not to the extent that a major improvement was apparent. In addition, the selected major hub for Republic was Minneapolis where they had formidable competition in the form of Northwest. Prior to the takeover of Republic by Northwest, Republic had improved its situation mostly through consolidation. It had lost market share in many western markets and decided to favour the central and eastern parts of the country.

Overall, the early experience with mergers was not favourable. This did not necessarily mean that mergers were not appropriate in the airline business. The timing of these mergers, just prior to the then impending recession of 1981–2, had a definite effect on their success. The carriers involved were still very vulnerable from the financial impacts of their acquisitions when they began losing traffic and yield due to the recession.

The new entrants compounded the problem by exacerbating the yield drop issue through their entry into many of Pan Am's domestic markets and those of the new Republic. This served to illustrate one of the great truths of the newly deregulated environment: the market was far less forgiving of error than it had previously been. A final illustration of the inadequacy of the initial carrier reactions to deregulation was to be found in their marketing tactics. Simply put, most of the large carriers practised a one P* marketing mix, price. Spurred by the need to expand market share in new markets, many carriers, even those with a high cost structure, felt the need to be competitive on price. It seemed that consumers were loyal to lowest price. In the era prior to the advent of frequent flier programmes and yield management systems, price was the key. Playing the fare wars with the new entrant, low-cost carriers became very expensive for the major carriers. As the general economy began to slide towards the recession in late 1981 and 1982 the major carriers began to show signs of financial stress, while the stronger of the new entrants began to show tripling of traffic growth. What was disappointing was that the major carriers had not the courage to charge more for a superior product. Product segmentation had not yet been implemented to any significant degree. It was not until the mid-1980s that the major

*One of four marketing Ps: product, place, price and promotion.

carriers began to innovate in product, distribution techniques and promotion. Once again this was a product of the bad habits developed in the regulated era when most of the marketing levers available to the carriers were controlled by the CAB.

The early experience

Overall, it is safe to say that most carriers were finding life to be very different. It may have been assumed by the politicians that the air transport industry had reached a state of maturity that would allow it to be left to its own devices, but the road to achieving an acceptable status in a freely competitive environment had been expensive for some. After the early years of deregulation a pattern of carrier

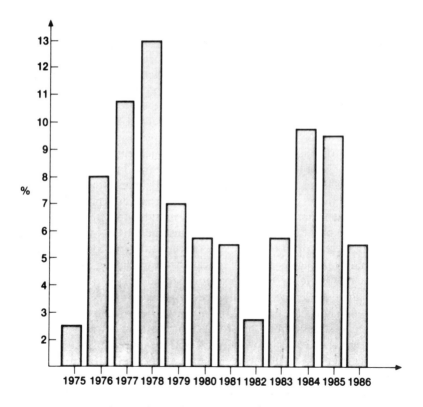

Figure 2.1 **US domestic carrier return on investment**
Source: **US ATA**

structures evolved which developed a certain predictability. The merging of existing carriers, and several types of new entrant carriers formed a clearly segmented industry that still exists today. Both the demands of the consumer and the general economic cycle have conspired to force carriers into a defined set of options.

The issue was that in a deregulated industry the carriers had had difficulty in defining anything constant about their situation. In fact the relatively large upheavals that were to take place in the 1981–2 recession served to demonstrate what will happen in the next recession now scheduled for early or mid-1989, depending on which forecasts one believes. It is in fact the putting into practice of the realization that air transportation in the US has become like any other domestic industry sector and thus is prone to the extremes of the economy. There are no economic regulations to impede the cyclical evolution that takes place in many other sectors. In fact the airlines have been thrust back into a corporate life-cycle that now provides for the extreme options of either succeeding or failing in a spectacular, and sometimes final, way. See Figs 2.1–2.3.

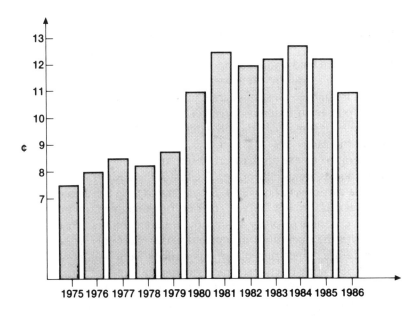

Figure 2.2 **US domestic carrier revenue per passenger mile (US/mile)**
Source: **US ATA**

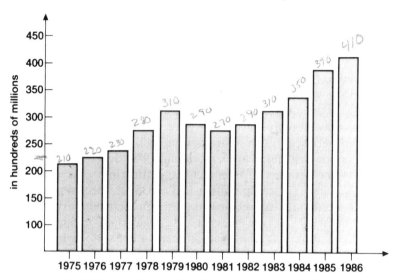

Figure 2.3   **US domestic scheduled passengers carried**
Source: **US ATA**

Modelling the competitive environment

In a turbulent and dynamic industry environment such as the US domestic airline industry, it may seem logical to assume that the only constant is change. This, of course, makes it difficult to plot longer-term responses to industry forces. There was, however, a certain pattern that did emerge in the US industry and it has remained true to form to this day.

In operating an existing carrier, or setting up a new entrant carrier, certain choices are usually made. The first is the desired segment into which the carrier is to be placed. Simply stated, one can create a high service carrier, a low service carrier or something in between. Another criterion revolves around the inherent relative costs associated with the operations of a given carrier. Secondly, in terms of cost there are a spectrum of options ranging from high cost to low cost carrier infrastructures. Each composite type of carrier has certain market behaviour patterns that are particularly favourable to their type of operation. Furthermore, each portion of the economic cycle, from peaks to troughs, represents a particularly advantageous period for one or the other type of carrier.

In basic terms, the US industry had evolved by 1980/81 into a

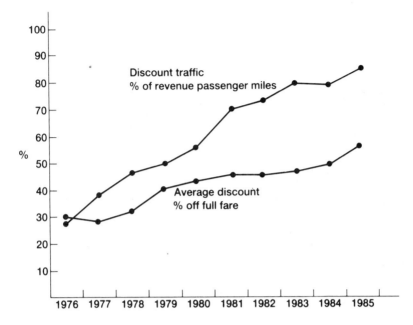

Figure 2.4 **Discount traffic on US major airlines**
***Source*: Air Transport Association of America**

market where three distinct types of carrier coexist (Fig. 2.6). The first is the high-cost/full-service carrier, the second is a low-cost/low-service carrier and the third is a hybrid with low cost and medium to high (differentiated) service levels. Each of these groups is dynamic in carrier membership and the relative gaps between types of carrier remain variable.

US domestic carrier types

The type 1 carrier is the high-cost/full-service carrier that many became used to in the days of regulation. These carriers were around in the pre-1978 era and in fact the complete lack of differentiation among scheduled carriers meant that almost every interstate US carrier was a type 1 airline. These carriers were characterized by high labour costs in combination with inflexible job tasks, high debt, low profitability, high fixed costs, a primary hub network strategy and an exclusive concentration on price competition in the first 2–3 years of deregulation. Carriers who fell into this category in 1982–3 were

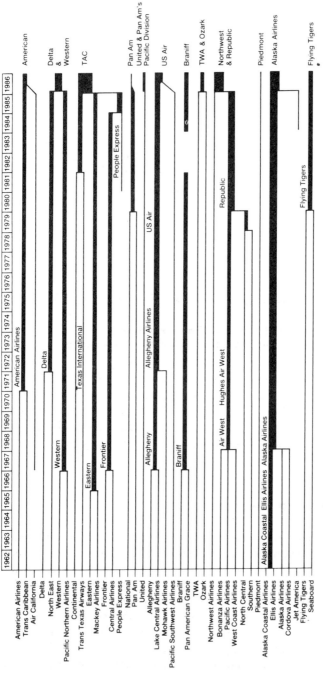

Figure 2.5 Consolidation of US airline industry
Source: Avmark Aviation Economist

Note: This chart illustrates the consolidation of individual US airlines over the past 25 years; the width of the lines does not reflect the relative importance of the airline groupings.

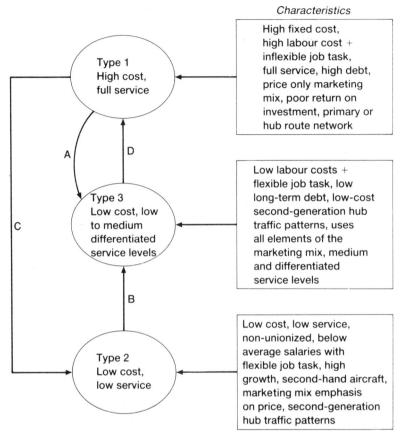

Characteristics

Type 1
High cost, full service

High fixed cost, high labour cost + inflexible job task, full service, high debt, price only marketing mix, poor return on investment, primary or hub route network

Type 3
Low cost, low to medium differentiated service levels

Low labour costs + flexible job task, low long-term debt, low-cost second-generation hub traffic patterns, uses all elements of the marketing mix, medium and differentiated service levels

Type 2
Low cost, low service

Low cost, low service, non-unionized, below average salaries with flexible job task, high growth, second-hand aircraft, marketing mix emphasis on price, second-generation hub traffic patterns

Figure 2.6 **US industry carrier types**

Eastern, Western, Pan Am, TWA, Continental, Frontier, United and Republic.

The type 2 carrier is the direct opposite of the type 1. It is characterized by low labour costs and flexible job tasks, low over-heads, relatively low debt, second-generation hubs, and a similar exclusive concentration on price as a marketing tool. The difference on price competition was that type 2s could afford to compete on price since their costs of operation were far lower than that of their major carrier type 1 competition. Carriers in this category were Midway (prior to the Midway–Metrolink conversion), People Express, New York Air, Altair (prior to bankruptcy), etc.

The last category, the type 3 carrier, is, as stated earlier, a hybrid group of carriers. This group is characterized by the low-cost operating structures of the type 2s with the full or differentiated product of the type 1s. The early members of this group were new entrant carriers who sought to maximize the positive spread between lower costs and the higher yields of the full service airline. See Fig. 2.7 for a comparison of costs.

Several carriers went directly into the type 3 group and met with limited success. Air Atlanta, Air One, Regent Air entered the market in the 1980s and were among others that tried and eventually failed. By entering the market as type 3, they had limited abilities to gain market presence for a variety of reasons. Many of these new entrants came into existence just after the worst of the 1981–2 recession when the major carriers were beginning to recover and were eager to squeeze out any competition in their higher yield segment. In addition, many of these type 3 carriers never got big enough to provide regular, dependable, high-frequency service on a large enough network of operations. There were two later categories of type 3 carrier, both of which joined the ranks of the type 3 carrier after having evolved from either type 1s or type 2s (evolutionary paths A and B on Figs. 2.3 and 2.8). The latter group is composed of carriers such as Midway that adopted the Midway–Metrolink concept of product segmentation after having been a simple type 2/Midway product. The Metrolink product provided a higher quality level of pre-, in- and- post-flight service and was more clearly targeted at the business traveller. The Metrolink concept retained the low cost, low overhead operating structure of its predecessor, Midway Airlines (the first new entrant after deregulation in 1978). While the Metro-link concept itself was not flawed, it did require a higher level of investment than Midway's previous type 2 product. The unfortunate coincidence was that Midway bought what was left of another new entrant, Air Florida, and the joint cash drain of financing that purchase when combined with the higher investment required to get Metrolink properly launched, caused Midway to revert to its previous role as a type 2 carrier. New York Air was another type 2 carrier that was part of the Lorenzo Texas Air Corp. group of carriers. In order to compete in the tough US eastern seabord short-haul commuter sectors (New York–Boston–Washington) it was felt that neither Texas International nor Continental had the cost structure to be successful new entrants in these markets. Therefore, New York Air was thrust into the market as a low-cost type 2 carrier in order to beat the incumbent players by charging lower fares and making money on lower yields. When the correct key product ingredients such as

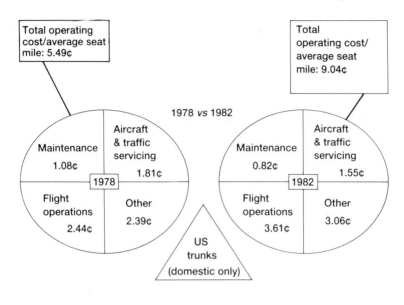

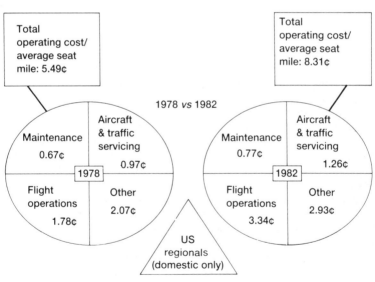

Figure 2.7 **Comparison of operating costs**
Source: **Eastern Airlines, 1982**

network spread, frequency of operation and price were in place, then New York Air added a higher level of service to their product mix. As such they attempted to match Eastern's product, beat their price and gain market penetration in the shuttle markets.

Strategic snapshot; Midway Airlines

(*Source: Lloyd's Aviation Economist*)

From type 2 to 3 and back again

Under stockholder pressure, Midway, the first new carrier to begin operating after the 1978 Air Deregulation Act, effectively abandoned, in early August 1985, its innovatory Metrolink strategy of specializing in the high yield business passenger sector and appears to be reverting to its original concept as a low cost carrier. Lawrence Hughes, vice president, marketing told *Lloyd's Aviation Economist* that Midway would now like to become 'the Southwest of the north-east'.

The company's DC-9-30s, operating on the Chicago/New York route, are being re-configured from 84 business seats to 94 seats, of which 24 are business and 70 coach. Services are being concentrated on Chicago/La Guardia instead of covering both La Guardia and Newark. A discounted fares programme, 'MetroMiser', is being introduced based on American's 'Ultimate Supersaver' programme, and an advertising campaign emphasizing price and frequency is underway.

Midway's Metrolink strategy appeared to be logical and sound. Yet similar strategies were adopted by Regent Air and Air One, both of which are now bankrupt, and Midway itself reported losses of $15m in 1983, $22m in 1984 and $7.7m in the first quarter of this year. Midway's recent decision has important implications for carriers like Air Atlanta and New York Air who must be wondering if the whole specialization concept is misguided.

At first (1979-mid-83), Midway used all the competitive tools of a new entrant, including a low cost and flexible labour force, cheap second-hand DC9s, a relatively low debt load and a bare bones pre-, in-, and post-flight product. And, because its operation was based at Midway airport, closer to downtown Chicago, than O'Hare, major carriers such as United found it difficult to respond to the newcomer's low fares without taking away traffic from its hub at O'Hare. Choosing to fly in a large volume market allowed Midway to steal small portions of passenger flow in individual sectors without attracting any significant competitive retaliation.

In essence, Midway served as a prototype for People Express although People Express chose routes where the lowest existing fare still considerably higher than those it was able to offer, serving places like Burlington (Vermont) and Buffalo (New York).

Segmentation in the US market
Traditional segmentation

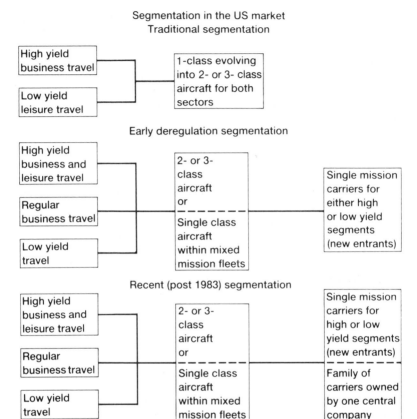

Early deregulation segmentation

Recent (post 1983) segmentation

In the early '80s when money was tight and corporate travel budgets continually under review, the low cost/low service market was healthy regardless of city pair traffic volumes. But when the economic situation improved, the cut cost operators suddenly found themselves under pressure.

At this point, Midway reversed its strategy by introducing its Metrolink concept. Operating between sophisticated large volume city pairs, Midway had to find the formula to enable it to meet the growing demands of the business traveller for convenience and comfort while maintaining its new entrant cost advantages.

The Metrolink concept went beyond segmentation of several classes of service on the same plane and beyond segmentation of part of a fleet to business services, to making the entire airline's mission that of catering to the business traveller.

This seemed to be complemented by the purchase of Air Florida assets and the setting-up of Midway Express (type 2), a second fully-segmented carrier in the Midway stable, serving south to north routes and catering mainly for leisure travellers.

Midway's originality extended to introducing a frequent user programme, a clever variation on the frequent flyer scheme which it also employed. Under this programme, a percentage of the money spent by businessmen using Metrolink was repaid directly the corporations who actually paid for the tickets.

According to Lawrence Hughes 'there were some merits in the old strategy but there was not enough time nor money to carry it out'. By focusing too narrowly on the business market, Midway Metrolink found that demand was too peaky, with businessmen preferring to fly either early morning or evening and always on weekdays. In addition, there was an excess of capacity on the Chicago–New York route.

It seems unlikely that changing to a low cost, conventional service operation will solve Midway's problems immediately (although Hughes says that Midway Metrolink will report a healthy second quarter profit). Much of its original cost advantage over the established carriers has disappeared, especially following the unionization of the pilots by Alpa, and the purchase of the Air Florida assets has eaten up a large amount of cash. In the end Midway reconsolidated itself into a single type 2, low cost, lower service type carrier that had experienced steady growth ever since.

Until recently New York Air was continuing to fulfil its role as a type 3 carrier in these high-density eastern seaboard commuter markets before it was sucked into the parent carrier, Continental. The third and last group of type 3 carriers was composed of the improved and leading carriers from the type 1 category. It could be argued that Delta, Northwest and American had been far enough ahead of their established carrier competition to have been practically considered as type 3s from 1978 on. Delta relied on its early and successful exploitation of the hub stragety, a non-unionized labour force that had equal if not better pay than the others but a more productive and flexible attitude towards job tasks, all of which was complemented by a solid balance sheet. American was in trouble during the early days of deregulation because of an old fleet, high labour costs and all of the other traditional maladies of the regulated carriers. They came to the forefront primarily on their ability to develop a strong marketing capability that included the awesome distribution strength of the SABRE computer reservations system. In fact, it was and still is true that the profits from SABRE are a fairly healthy cross-subsidy facility for the airline. The development of the Dallas–Fort Worth hub, after American's move from New York, also helped improve the carriers' position. Finally, Northwest was recognized as the meanest carrier around with an ultra-conservative financially-based management style. When going into the uncertainties of the newly deregulated environment and an impending recession, one could argue that this may have been the best possible management style to adopt. Northwest had virtually no long-term debt. Financial management, along with a very tough attitude towards organized labour, helped keep Northwest's costs the lowest of the big established carriers. Despite a number of strikes, Northwest had managed to keep the lid on labour costs. In the pre-deregulation days, the lower operating costs of Northwest had been necessary in order to compete with Pacific Rim carriers with which they had been battling for years. When deregulation was adopted in 1978, the lower operating costs were a blessing for the Northwest domestic route network as well. So these three carriers were in the forefront when deregulation struck, whether they had planned it or not. Having a head start in what was to become recognized as the right direction helped Delta, Northwest and American become the first three older carriers to enter the type 3 category.

The identification of these three distinct types of carrier, originally done in 1984, was only part of the story, however. Using these three categories it became possible to project, with a fair degree of accuracy, the strategic options open to various carriers or categories of carrier. As US carriers were just beginning to get used to a deregulated environment they were forced to deal with a more serious obstacle to their individual survival, their first recession since being liberated from the protective cocoon of CAB regulation. This was to.be a challenge and learning experience that would cost the industry billions of dollars and some carriers their corporate lives. It was to be the most serious threat the industry had faced, topping even the previous oil crises. Following the evolutionary model (see Fig. 2.8), the most vulnerable category of carrier was the type 1. Carriers in this group had to find ways to cut costs, repair aging products, networks, fleets and market shares. Inevitably, any action on the latter four issues ended up creating an adverse impact on cost reduction. When attempting to move out of the type 1 group, there were two options: becoming a type 2 or a type 3. A key related concern was the speed with which the move should be accomplished. The speed of change was often conditioned by the perception of how long market survival was possible under a *status quo* regime. There are several examples of attempts to migrate away from type 1 status.

Clearly the most drastic of these examples was the Continental

Chapter 11* strategy. By having ownership of Texas International and Continental Airlines, Frank Lorenzo was presiding over a financial disaster. Losses were in tens of millions per quarter and despite the relatively acceptable performance of the international portion of the Continental network the losses from domestic operations were dragging the whole carrier down. Had the *status quo* been allowed to continue it became clear that financial trouble would claim Continental before the recession had let up. Time was of the essence.

Taking advantage of the protective covenants of the Chapter 11 bankruptcy procedures, Lorenzo accomplished a near 50 per cent reduction in many costs (specifically labour costs) in the space of a weekend. It was postured that this cost reduction was essential to the continued survival of the carrier and it probably was. As a comparative measure, it should be noted that it took Braniff many months (24 plus) to restart operations subsequent to the declaration of Chapter 11 bankruptcy. It should not, however, be assumed that the restructuring process at Continental was painless, least of all for the workforce. With hindsight, it seems clear that this was a key part of Continental's resuscitation strategy. In looking at Fig. 2.8, Continental followed path C from a type 1 to a type 2 carrier. This allowed it to take advantage of its size and network which, when combined with its new-found low-cost operating characteristic, made Continental the largest type 2 carrier in the US industry. Sub-strategies used to accomplish this approach to change include subsidiary spin-off, asset stripping and, of course, the once popular Chapter 11 bankruptcy proceeding. (The impact of the Chapter 11 bankruptcy statute has been limited by the so-called 'Lorenzo Amendment' that attempts to reduce management rights in curtailing union benefits.) Continental is using the asset stripping strategy in its current battle to trim costs at Eastern. The shifting of aircraft and routes away from the Eastern unit of Texas Air Corporation over to the Continental operating unit is designed to encourage labour to agree to reducing Eastern's rather onerous cost structure. Continental also used the subsidiary spin-off strategy when, as previously discussed, it created New York Air with a specific geographic and market type business strategy.

The second evolutionary path to be followed was path A. This approach to change implied a much more gradual time period and

*Chapter 11 - a protective bankruptcy statute that prevents creditors from seizing assets immediately. The company can continue as long as they have a valid business plan approved by the Courts.

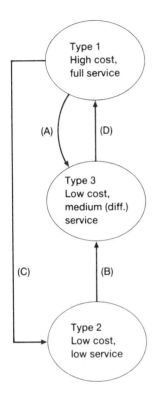

(A) This path is followed by healthy, traditional carriers. It requires preparation and even those carrier managements that realized change was required before 1978 still needed a long time to move to a type 3. Carriers choosing this path have traditionally been financially and strategically conservative

(B) Followed by born or reborn carriers (post-1978). Low-cost carriers that grow and those with clearly defined market segmentation follow this path

(C) Followed by airlines that do not have time to follow path A. This path usually causes a great deal of dislocation. Strategies consist of one or more of: asset stripping, chapter 11, subsidiary spin-off. These and other methods may conspire to create low-cost carriers which can in turn compete with other type 2 and type 3 airlines

(D) A path followed by carriers whose costs grow much more rapidly than those of the competition

Figure 2.8 **Evolutionary paths**

was the path that many established carriers tried to follow. By negotiating new, less costly wage deals with their workforces and trimming costs wherever possible, this group of type 1 airlines tried to join the more efficient group of type 3 airlines. A third evolutionary path was that followed by both Midway and New York Air when they migrated from type 2 to type 3 carrier status.

As previously mentioned, this path simply involves maintaining the type 2 low-cost structure that was previously in place and at the same time enhancing the pre-, in- and post-flight product offered to customers. In this way the type 1s, who were fighting to become more efficient and productive, and the type 2s, seeking to grow not only in terms of network size but also in terms of participating in a variety of market segments (high and low yield), met at the type 3 carrier structure. It seemed that the type 3 was the common ground to which most carriers aspired. This trend is conditioned by the portion of the economic cycle at which the industry finds itself at any given time. Having established the types of carrier and the potential ways in which they evolve, the final step is to simulate how the interactions will occur as the economic cycle progresses from good to bad and back again. As US domestic air transport was unleashed from the artificially stable environment of intense economic regulation, it should be noted that the market players began to exhibit a variety of reactions. Are they explainable or even predictable?

Carrier types and the economic cycle

One would assume that a recession, or near depression, as occurred in the US in the early 1980s would be bad news for all airlines. In looking at the carrier results, it can be seen that this was not true. It tended to be the larger, established carriers that had the most trouble. In fact, the smaller new carriers seemed to prosper with many posting over 100 per cent growth rates. It is true that one of the unexpected consequences of deregulation has been that not all carriers now have to face an economic downturn with a sense of impending doom. Similarly, not all types of carrier face the economic upturn with an equal sense of excitement. In fact, various types of carrier are strong or weak relative to each other at different points in the economic cycle. These inherent, structural factors cannot be ignored since they do affect various types of carrier structure depending upon timing and whether the carrier is a type 1, 2 or 3 airline. From these assumptions flow a concept that each of these types of airline has a zone of vulnerability as it does a zone of strength.

Zones of vulnerability (Fig. 2.9)

Starting with the type 1 carrier, we note that the downturn and pit of the economic cycle represent the worst operating period for this group. This is a rather conventional expectation since most firms in most lines of business have a harder time during the recessionary phase. In the downturn and pit, the high-cost, full-service type 1

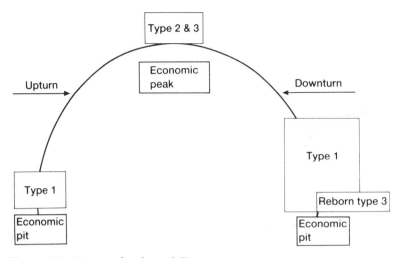

Figure 2.9 **Zones of vulnerability**

cannot defray costs by growing since the market is invariably contracting at this point. In addition, the overhead structures type 1s build up during the good years cost them a lot to retain. Large maintenance structures, in particular, are often underutilized as type 1s dump aircraft in order to consolidate and cut costs. Since it is difficult to cut off 20–30 per cent of a maintenance hangar, the type 1s invariably grant indirect help to their low-cost type 2 competition by selling them underutilized maintenance capacity at bargain rates. This in turn means that the type 2s can avoid setting up most of the maintenance structure (hangars and facilities) within their own airline. Airport terminals, slots and gates are also sold off to the growing type 2 and 3 carriers during this phase. The timing of fleet acquisition and disposal has a critical effect on the relative strength of the carrier types. In downturns, the type 2 and 3 carriers can pick up second-hand aircraft at bargain prices, as the type 1s are forced to unload excess capacity. These aircraft then represent an advantage that can be used for the rest of the recession and into the next cycle. This gives type 2s and new entrant type 3s a structural advantage over type 1s and type 1s who are reborn as type 3s after having followed evolutionary path A. The negative impact is compounded by the fact that type 1s and reborn type 3s tend to purchase new aircraft at or near the peak, when things are going well, and take delivery during the downturn and pit . This means, of course, that the type 1s and re-born 3s are making heavy lease and/or mortgage payments when they can least afford to, during the recessionary phase. For type 2s and the original type 3s, on the other hand, the zone of vulnerability includes the top half of the upside and the peak of the economic cycle. At these phases, the higher cost operators can use the same tactics that they employed in the regulated market. Table 2.6 shows a sample of carrier evolution between types.

These tactics included domination of the distribution chains, through expensive computer reservations systems, purchase of more efficient aircraft and control of gates and slots at key airports. All these upside and peak-oriented strategies depend on growth in the market. Increasing revenues enable the type 1s and reborn type 3s to

Table 2.6 A sample of carrier evolution between types

1980		1985	
Type 1		**Type 1**	
Eastern	Northwest	Eastern	Frontier
Delta	Republic	US Air	
US Air	Piedmont	Republic	
Continental	Frontier	Western	
Ozark	American	Ozark	
TWA	Braniff	Pan Am	
Pan Am	Western	TWA	
1980–4.		1985	
Type 2		**Type 2**	
People Express		People Express	
Altair		Braniff	
New York Air		Continental	
Midway		Presidential	
Frontier Horizon			
Type 3		**Type 3**	
Southwest		Southwest	(O)*
Midway Metrolink		Midway	(RB)†
Air Atlanta		Air Atlanta	(O)
Air One		Delta	(RB)
		New York Air	(RB)
		Northwest	(RB)
		American	(RB)

* Denotes carriers that were born as type 3 carriers in their original form (lower cost base, medium and differentiated product).
† Denotes carriers that were either type 1s or type 2s at the start of deregulation and have since evolved into type 3s.

expand into new sectors and use their sheer size to conquer the smaller competition. During the upturn and the peak the bigger carriers can afford to go after all sectors and undertake more vigorous fare wars with a greater chance of success, resulting in fights with smaller carriers for even 1 or 2 per cent market shares. At other points in the cycle, the type 1s and reborn type 3s cannot afford to segment their operations to the extent necessary to compete with original type 3s which have specialized in an all-business or similar operating format using a low-cost operating base. This set of forces has been largely responsible for the problems that were faced by type 3s like Midway, Air One and New York Air in late 1985. All of a sudden these carriers were being actively pursued by larger carriers who were gaining back their market strength and able to compete for

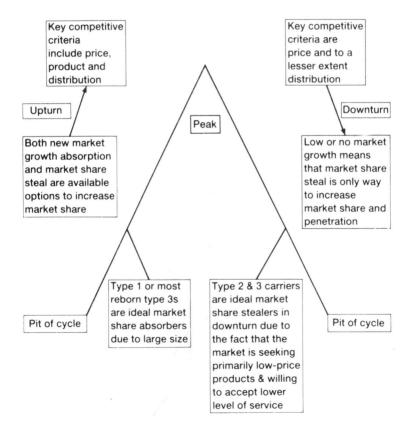

Figure 2.10 **Cyclical market characteristics**

customer loyalty using expensive but effective and attractive frequent flier programmes. It is a fact that these larger type 1s and reborn 3s are and will continue to be better growth absorbers in the upturn and peak than the smaller former new entrants are, simply because of their size and resultant market and network synergy (see Fig. 2.10). In addition, the factors of production that had been so cheap and readily available to the type 2s and type 3s during the recessionary phase had all but disappeared. Cheap trained labour, second-hand aircraft, cheap gates and slots were no longer available. For this reason Texas Air, among others, had to start buying new aircraft for its member carriers – a move that was expensive and will hurt Continental's costs in the next downturn. Finally, the huge capacity of the type 1s and reborn 3s to generate cash during the upturn of the cycle is a key factor in determining their decided strength over other types. It is one of the prime reasons why merger fever has emerged, again, as a popular strategy during late 1985, 1986 and 1987. It is equally clear that in the downturn and pit of the economic cycle the dynamic and lower cost type 2s and 3s are better market share stealers than the larger type 1s and ex-type 1s now turned type 3s.

Gaining market size becomes crucial because during the upturn and peak of the economic cycle, the larger the carrier the larger the synergy, network and market share. This in turn means that market growth absorption is facilitated for the type 1s and reborn type 3s.

The reversal of the prevailing economic scenario serves to negate size because it is often less efficient in a declining market. That is why mergers between medium and large sized carriers are less successful in the downturn and pit of the cycle and why the bigger, higher cost type 1 carriers find that the same synergy of size that stood them in good stead during market growth has betrayed them in the downturn. This rollercoaster effect of size that provides huge sums of operating cash flows in the upturn/peak often leads to large cash flow operating deficits in the downturn/pit. This weakening of the larger type 1s and ex-type 1s (now type 3s) often gives their smaller competitors the breathing space they require to grow, primarily through market share steal. The trick is that the new entrants must grow fast enough to have comparable synergy before the next peak arrives; otherwise they are at a real competitive disadvantage. Of all the new entrants since 1978, only the Texas Air Group was able to make the transformation from new entrant to large carrier in the period between the economic pit of 1982 and the upturn/peak in the late 1980s. As a result, the Texas Air Group of carriers are the only major new entrants left in the US domestic market. All of the other

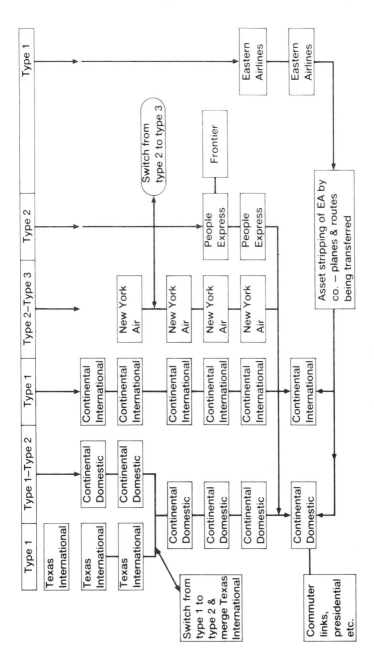

Figure 2.11 **The evolution of Texas Air Corporation**

remaining new entrants are segmented either by geographically regionalized networks or by product. The Texas Air Group achieved their size and synergy not through internally generated growth but through acquisition and merger (see Fig. 2.11). By combining the remains of the debt-ridden Continental, Texas International, New York Air and People Express (Frontier as a part of People Express), and later Eastern Airlines, Continental was able to achieve the synergy of size fast enough to retain a major part of the market. This was not achieved without dislocation to employees and has resulted in a conglomerate carrier that is not out of trouble yet. Continental still has to worry about $3.9 billion of debt among other things. Figure 2.12 illustrates survival strategies for new entrants.

The experience of the last economic cycle poses the following question: can any new entrant get big enough by itself to become a significant and sustained (long-term) competitor in the industry? The last cycle shows that the only carrier that is still around is composed of two of the weaker former type 1s (Continental, Eastern), the largest of the new entrants, People Express, plus three smaller carriers of various lineage (New York Air, Frontier and Texas International). The fact that the weaker ones were absorbed into a bigger, hybrid carrier (composed of type 1, 2 and 3s) illustrates the

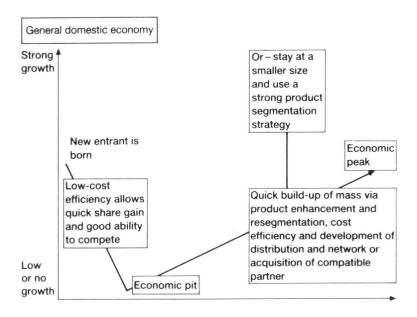

Figure 2.12 **New entrant survival characteristics**

survival of the fittest. In the next economic downturn, it can be expected that a new crop of weaker type 1s will be absorbed into another growing carrier. The difference is that in the next economic downturn, the second since US domestic deregulation, the prevailing cost structure gap between new entrants and the established carriers will be less than in the previous recession. The larger carriers of type 1 structure will be more efficient than their predecessors were in 1981–2. Therefore, the competitive dislocation will be diminished. This trend towards increasing industry stability through all phases of the economic cycle should continue unabated until a point is reached, in the fourth or fifth economic cycle since deregulation, when the cyclical regeneration of new entrant competitive carriers will be greatly reduced (see Fig. 2.13). At that point the incumbent carriers will have developed the flexibility to remain relatively cost and service competitive through the downturn and upturn of the cycle. Because of these more flexible and healthier carriers, the barriers to new entrants will be greatly increased. This is not to say, however,

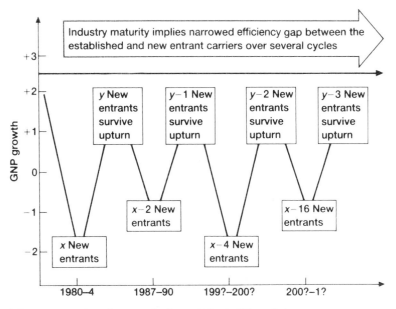

Figure 2.13 **US industry evolution**

that new entrants will not continue to enter the market, especially during the downturn and pit of the cycle. Amusingly, one could speculate that once the US domestic industry has reached this point of relative stability (oligopoly) the politicians might try to re-regulate the business in order to provide more equal access to markets for smaller carriers. It is commonly known that the re-regulation of access to limited airway and airport infrastructures is a potential solution to the artificial barriers to entry now blocking smaller carrier access to these airports. In 10–15 years time could incumbent carrier size represent another inequity in the system? Figure 2.14 shows the number of US airlines in 1978–87.

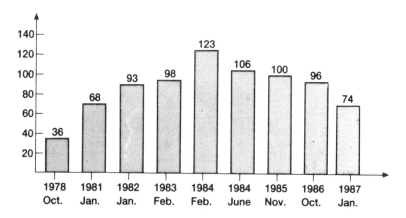

Figure 2.14 **Number of US scheduled airlines (operating under section 401 certificate)**
Source: **Airline Economics, Inc.**

Strategic snapshot: Presidential Airlines

(*Source: Lloyd's Aviation Economist May 1986*)

When not to start up a new entrant (originally written in April 1986)

Presidential Airways stands out from the many other new entrants to the US domestic market because, during its original incarnation, the airline had chosen an original combination of strategies.

Using the 1, 2, 3 type model, one was able to analyse the then present and potential future of Presidential.

Since the debut of US deregulation carriers have evolved between these various categories of carrier. A fallout of this evolution has been the subsegmentation with the type 3 category, the fastest growing of the three.

This segment has typically been composed of original type 3 airlines such as Air Atlanta and New York Air and the re-born type 3s, which have been recycled from the type 1 category, such as Delta, American and Northwest. Now there has emerged a third subcategory of type 3 carrier. Presidential typified this new group which basically sought to meld the best strategies of the previous two subsegments of the type 3 (see diagram on page 68).

The new type 3s, labelled the boom-babies, are those whose recent birth (1986) (into new entrant status) has pitted them against the most difficult to penetrate air travel market since deregulation. The re-born type 3s are growing larger by the hour, whether by acquisition or internal growth, and the chances of a new carrier striking out on a successful and independent course are much reduced compared to 18 or 24 months ago (during the 1982-3 recession). As such, many of those who have recently tried to be a new entrant type 2 or type 3 have met with Chapter 11 bankruptcy or worse.

Since the US domestic economic cycle was on the upswing (1986), it seemed normal to expect that certain carrier types would be in an advantageous position. In fact, the categories that seem to be benefiting the most are the bigger type 2s and the re-born type 3s. Due to their market size and attendant synergy they are gaining dominant market positions. Against this background the tiny new upstart, Presidential Airways, had begun its hopeful trek towards success. How did they plan on attaining this goal which had been unreachable for so many others?

Presidential was conceived under rather unusual circumstances in that its management is composed mainly of ex-People Express personnel—new entrant spawning another new entrant. Normally, it is the established carriers that lend their personnel to newly created carriers.

Presidential falls under a growing category of new entrants which could be called 'vendetta carriers'. This group consists of airlines founded by former disgruntled employees of competing carriers. It counts, for instance, Lamar Muse as one of its early members. His breaking away from Southwest to form his own carrier was seen as a way of expressing dissatisfaction at being dumped by Southwest. But Muse Air no longer exists, having been bought out by Southwest and re-named TransStar Airlines. A recent casualty in the same category is the group that broke away from Continental to form Pride Airlines. Presently mired in Chapter 11, the future for Pride seems bleak especially since it was operationally active for only a matter of weeks.

Taking these examples one wonders whether being a member of the 'vendetta carriers' group is a good thing. However, Presidential's corporate pysche does not seem to include direct competitive retaliation against People Express.

In fact, Presidential adopted the type 3 operating format which included a regular bundle of passenger amenities, including advance booking and seat selection and first class (8 first-class/111 coach seats) on all flights. It has chosen a perfected hub and spoke concept, using what was an underutilized airport (Dulles in Washington) as a hub for its operations which were primarily north-south routes on the US eastern seaboard. Presidential's fleet comprised five leased second-hand 737-200 aircraft.

The company used a modified flexible job task concept that allowed for cross-utilization of employees in various functions. The non-unionized work force had also purchased carrier shares which, if all had gone according to plan, would have provided a good return to the employee-investors.

So far, it all sounds very familiar and leads the analyst to question whether there was room for another type 3 in the US air transport market. At this point, however, the Presidential story begins to deviate from the norm set by previous type 3 new entrants such as New York Air and Air Atlanta.

The overall image conveyed by previous new entrants, whether type 2 or 3, was one of independence. They sought to differentiate themselves from the typical strategies used by their bigger type 1 and re-born type 3 competitors. In contrast, Presidential seized upon an alliance strategy almost from the very beginning. It originally announced schedule and marketing co-ordination with Pan Am at Dulles and went on to explore purchasing an interest in commuter carriers and carrier code sharing with others. Finally, Presidential had been courting both United and American in order to find an ideal mainline domestic feed partner, though nothing concrete came from this early on.

SUBCATEGORISATION OF TYPE 3 CARRIERS

RE-BORN TYPE 3 ('BLUE CHIPPERS', evolved from Type 1)	ORIGINAL TYPE 3 (NEW ENTRANTS, evolved from Type 2)	NEW TYPE 3 ('BOOM BABIES', no previous group affinity)
• New aircraft	• Used + new aircraft	• Used narrowbody aircraft (frequently subletted to charter carriers at weekends)
• Commuter feed		• All level feed (early alliances)
• Significant market presence	• Small segmented market presence	• Small segmented market presence
• High infrastructure (airport) costs	• Low infrastructure (airport) costs	• Medium infrastructure (airport) costs
• Medium to high labour/operating costs	• Low labour/ operating costs	• Low labour/ operating costs
• First or second generation multi-hub operations	• Single or dual second-generation hub operations	• Single second-generation hub operations (frequently buying own terminal)
• Full service product	• Medium to full service product	• Medium to full service product
• Restricted price wars	• Good price competitor	• Frequent flyer program at start-up

The ultimate aim would be to plug Presidential into a network with international, mainline domestic and commuter links, thus positioning it to obtain feed from all three levels of carrier traffic. It seemed that Presidential's management was seeking to survive through acquiring traffic links wherever possible and it was putting this motive ahead of any retaliatory action against People Express.

However, United decided that it too would set up its own hub at Dulles and serve 50 cities from there. Since the Dulles hub would, in large part, represent new growth for United, it meant that the carrier would be able to deploy cheaper factors of production to operate the hub.

If United can isolate older (fully depreciated and paid off) 737s and utilize new, entry level cheaper labour (lower of the two-tier wage scale) to run the Dulles operation, this will significantly improve United's ability to compete on low unrestricted fares with the type 3 carriers at Dulles.

In addition, fellow type 3 competitor, New York Air, was also beefing up services and giving Presidential direct price competition on many routes. Since New York Air was part of the growing Texas Air group (Continental, People Express, Frontier and Eastern), this gave New York Air more staying power in a head-to-head price war with Presidential.

Presidential was therefore faced with a large degree of potentially damaging competition. By talking to American Airlines, Presidential may simply have been trying to get United's co-operation in order to prevent American from coming to Dulles and providing more competition than this, still underutilized, airport could have handled. And, by playing one off against the other, Presidential may become a willing pawn in the all consuming battle between United and American for dominance.

The final outcome of this strategy could have been that either United or American would buy out Presidential and use it as a low cost operating division of their respective operations. This would, no doubt, yield a healthy return for the present owners even though it would represent a departure from present strategies for United or American (growth through internal means).

Other large carrier strategies which Presidential has made use of from its inception include having a frequent flyer programme based on a points/trip rather than a mileage concept. The major attraction of frequent flyer programmes is the list of vacation destinations offered to the airline passengers. This is where the new entrants have tradionally had trouble keeping up with the big carriers and their many exotic destinations. Florida is as exotic as Presidential gets in terms of vacation destinations for reward winners. So, the airline has a limited appeal compared with other carriers.

Unlike other smaller new entrant airlines, Presidential has so far not chosen to adopt the corporate user scheme which seeks to reward the corporation which pays for the flying as opposed to the individual doing the flying. It may just be that reducing the cost of travel (through some bulk-buy mechanism) for corporations using Presidential will be more beneficial in terms of stimulating longer corporate travel loyalty in the airline's mostly business-orientated markets.

Smaller carriers can afford to do this since their stake, in percentage share terms, in the business travel market is relatively small. Conversely, the larger carriers would be reluctant to implement parallel programmes because of the cost implications on much larger network systems.

An additional big carrier strategy employed by Presidential was ownership of airport infrastructure. By building its own mid-field terminal at Dulles, it had added $4.5m to its overhead costs. Guaranteed gate space (10 gates at the Presidential terminal) and the ability to control hub operations were key advantages but, when traded off against other start-up costs, one wonders whether Presidential needed to do this as a part of its first phase of operations.

There are complicating factors present at Dulles which could explain why Presidential needed its own facility. These include the fact that the only mode

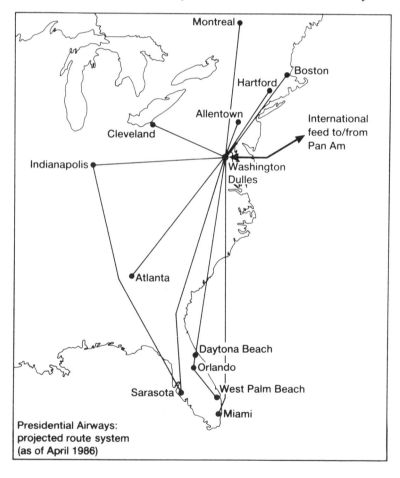

Presidential Airways:
projected route system
(as of April 1986)

of pasenger handling at that time included Passenger Transfer Vehicles which make hub type scheduling with 20-30 minute connections between flights, in any given departure and arrival bank, difficult. A further benefit could be the opportunity to sub-lease gate space in the future. Still, with small numbers of daily flights in their original schedule, Presidential may not have come up against trouble in this area for 8-12 months after service start-up, and the funds used here could have leased additional aircraft or extended Presidential's staying power in a price war.

Where does all this place Presidential? Would this hybrid collection of strategies stand Presidential in good stead throughout all phases of economic cycle?

Although Presidential aimed for a respectable 5.7 cents/ASM post-start-up operating cost, the fixed cost overheads were higher at Presidential than at some of its other type 2 or 3 competition. To its credit Presidential had not let potential membership in the 'vendetta carriers' club destroy its commercial integrity. However, there does seem to be a residue of People Express thought process left among senior management. Could it be, in their minds, that they are really building Terminal C in Newark for a previous employer as opposed to a high overhead terminal facility for an embryonic Presidential at Dulles?

Initial attempts at purchasing commuter feed had recently gone sour in a termination of the Presidential/Gull Airways transaction, leaving Presidential to continue its search for commuter feed. This did not detract from the correctness of the alliance strategy which Presidential seemed to have adopted, but implementation could prove difficult due to the ever shortening list of potential partners.

Building terminals or having frequent flier programmes are items that previous successful new entrants did not indulge in until several years after their founding. Because of the more difficult air travel markets of late 1985 and 1986 Presidential may have felt forced to introduce what they considered to be all of their optimal bundle of strategies right away and make full impact on the market. The issue then becomes whether they have the financial staying power to reap the longer term benefits.

Although Presidential was probably one of the better capitalized new entrants, and benefited from a mature, efficient management team, it has a strategy that was expensive to implement. In the final analysis, Presidential was born too late into the cycle to expect an independent future. It eventually became a commuter carrier for United and then switched to become a commuter partner for another US major carrier. Should it survive through to the downside of the next cycle, it may once again become an independent force in the market. Interestingly, there have been no successful major jet carrier new entrants since then.

As the upturn and peak of the economy arrive, the words 'customer service' take on new importance. When discussing the new

Delta advertising campaign, Mr W Hawkins, Sr VP Marketing at Delta, said: 'the campaign focuses on personal service, which is the single most important reason people choose one airline over another, since fares and equipment are at parity' (in the upturn and peak of the economic cycle). Large segments of the market no longer look at price as the only criterion and are in fact willing to pay for better service. The large, low-cost Texas Air Group of carriers were far behind their established contemporaries in this area. In fact, Continental must now denigrate its low-cost structure to add large chunks of overhead costs in order to support better customer service within its airlines. Another carrier that took early advantage of this swing in consumer preference was People Express. By providing no frills at the right time they achieved phenomenal growth in the pit and recessionary phase. Paradoxically, it was their ignorance of the impact of abandoning their chosen segment that was one of the key downfalls of PE on their way to being absorbed by the Texas Air Group.

Clearly the different phases of the cycle constitute different zones of vulnerability for the respective carrier types. Even so, some carriers do try to bridge the gap with hybrid strategies designed to borrow on the strengths of another type of carrier. America West, which went rapidly from a type 2 to type 3 in its early history, decided to sign a feed agreement with Northwest at Phoenix. Even though the agreement has since lapsed it was entered into at a critical point along America West's growth curve, the fledgling stage when resilience to large carrier competition is at its lowest ebb. Northwest was in fact a competitor of America West in earlier times, in addition to being an obstruction in their quest to obtain a dominant share of the Phoenix hub market (something America West now has). By having the feed agreement, America West freed Northwest to fight competitive battles in other markets while providing traffic feed to critical longer haul European and Asian routes to the Northwest system network. It also allowed America West to build up strength at Phoenix. After the agreement was de-activated, America West kept its market advantage. From the concepts of zones of vulnerability, several complementary sub-strategies can be developed. The key concept which cannot be forgotten is that every point in the economic cycle has its peculiar and specific characteristics. Different types of carrier do better at different times and none do inherently well at all phases of the cycle. Ignoring these factors will automatically place a carrier at an initial disadvantage when compared to airlines who observe these 'rules of the air'.

When to grow

For the type 1s the time to exert their strength is during the upturn and peak of the economic cycle (See Fig. 2.15). Carriers such as Northwest, Delta, American and United have all been playing this strategy since late 1985. Despite the fact that the economic cycle was against it, People Express decided to go against the normal strategy for a type 2 at the peak (consolidation) and bought Frontier. This was another of the factors that led to the ultimate demise of People Express. Despite the fact that in late 1985 People Express' costs were relatively low, they soon grew quickly due to (1) the Frontier purchase, (2) the dearth of second-hand aircraft and (3) the increasing costs of labour. The signs of corporate discomfort began to emerge when People Express started raising fares with little inflationary justification in late 1985. The decreased pace of growth after mid-1985 could have been the justification for the purchase of Frontier.

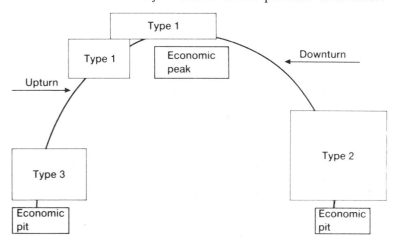

Figure 2.15 **Ideal phases for carrier growth**

Strategic snapshot: People Express

(*Source: The Avmark Aviation Economist January 1987*)

Post-mortem: the type 2 that forgot to consolidate at the right time

What happened to People Express? One answer is that the early advantages People Express enjoyed were negated by the upturn in the

US economy. Moreover, People Express management made the wrong strategic responses to the changed circumstances.

Factors of production

The birth and subsequent growth of People Express was heavily dependent on the severity of the recession. The recession helped its major carrier competition lose millions of dollars, shed trained airline staff, cut back on routes and sell off plenty of second-hand aircraft. Once the majors had sold aircraft they began looking for contract maintenance work in order to keep utilization high at technical facilities. People Express took advantage of these favourable rates for maintenance as well.

As the impact of the recession lessened, the supply of cheap second-hand aircraft dried up and the previously laid off employees were absorbed back. People Express lost the inherent advantages it had known as a low cost, low service carrier earlier in the decade.

Human resources

During the recession many had gone to work for People Express because they had been laid off from other carriers; others worked there because it was an exciting, high-profile company. Twenty-four short months ago People Express was placing full page advertisements in the *New York Times* telling anyone interested to come to a seminar at a local hotel and promising that the hiring of hundreds would result. Where have those times gone?

During the recession People Express was growing rapidly and experiencing a healthy rise in its stock price. Contrary to the prevailing practice at larger carriers, People Express had flexible remuneration mechanisms. Low base salaries for its non-unionized staff seemed acceptable to most employees during a recession as the difference could be made up through profit sharing and stock options.

Over the past 12-14 months, while People Express was facing its toughest direct competition ever, it had to contend with employee disatisfaction and eventually requests for rises in base salary. This was to compensate for the profits they were not sharing in and the stock they owned that was not appreciating.

Again a change in the economic cycle from pit to near-peak helped reverse a previously advantageous situation. Even Don Burr was saying, in late 1985, that '1986 was to be a year of consolidation'. But, while People Express should have been becoming more efficient in the face of heightened competition, its costs of operation were actually rising.

The buy-out of Frontier, a unionized carrier, was not a very positive stimulus. Getting unionized employees to accept the lower People Express pay scales, or worse, bringing People Express staff up to Frontier levels would have been difficult to swallow.

Market strategy

In the early days, the market strategy for People Express was simple. It entered markets with relatively little competition where the lowest prevailing fare was still quite high. Using its lower cost/seat mile advantage People Express charged low fares and made money by attracting higher volumes of traffic.

Also, in these markets, was traffic shifted from other modes of transport. From places like Burlington, Vermont to Newark it was cheaper to fly on People Express, than to travel on Amtrak or the bus.

As the majors recovered and began re-entering many markets People Express began to feel increased competition in its own markets. The staying power of the majors in fare wars was greatly enchanced now that they were not losing many millions of dollars every quarter, as they had been during the pit of the recession. People Express itself had expanded to the point where the number of remaining growth markets in which it could exploit its cost advantages dwindled significantly. The outcome was that a carrier dependent on high levels of growth to successfully continue its strategies was experiencing a drastic slow-down in growth.

The final significant factor that affected the carrier was a change in consumer preferences. The overall market is predisposed to full-service carriers when the general economy is healthy. Business travellers persuaded their companies to let them back into the business and first class cabins of the major carriers (see Fig. 2.16).

Similarly, many leisure travellers turned away from People Express when the majors began offering capacity-restricted discount fares. In many instances, these fares matched People Express while providing the many amenities that passengers had come to expect in better times.

No frills service, poor on-time performance and unrestricted low fares have always been part of the People Express product. Changing these perceptions in consumers' minds proved impossible.

Growth and acquisition

People Express' strategy for growth had always been one of growing from within instead of through acquisition. Unfortunately, it ignored its traditional 'contrary cycle of strategies' and joined in the acquisition game. The result was the ill-fated acquisition of Frontier. Frontier cost $10m of losses per month in the last months People Express operated it.

As in its own operations, People Express adopted a schizophrenic approach to segmentation at Frontier. First, it tried to make Frontier a no-frills carrier like itself, so turning off traditional Frontier customers who had come to expect full service. Then it restructured and re-made Frontier a full-service carrier while announcing that it was also going to turn itself into a full-service business travel airline. The market just could not keep up with PE.

The Frontier decision and the lack of consistency in marketing/product strategy decision-making were the final nails in the coffin.

Unfortunately, the cost of market expansion through Frontier and an attempt to build a Denver hub proved very difficult and costly for People Express. In fact during this period People Express broke many of the simple rules that a type 2 must follow when the upturn and peak of the economic cycle are present. They bought terminals, tried to develop a computer system, built up a maintenance infrastructure and acquired a carrier with a high-cost operating structure including a unionized labour force (Frontier). People Express went contrary to many of the rules dictated by the environment and ended up paying heavily for it later on. In fact in the next downturn, even if People Express had survived the last cycle, they would no longer have been the barebones type 2 carrier they once were. There would, no doubt, have been another newly dedicated low-cost carrier that would have challenged for type 2 supremacy. By contrast, carriers such as American, Delta and Northwest have been practising the tactics of market dominance that they have become used to. The tools they are using to compete among themselves include international market expansion, CRS distribution system dominance, frequent flier programmes (even though they all admit this is becoming an expensive item, none seems willing to stop these programmes), high technology fleet acquisition, fare matching wars, expansion of existing hubs and the addition of new 'mini-hubs', etc. It cannot be denied that the survivors of the last recession have become more efficient and effective in the practice of market dominance techniques. The question remains: how will these carriers fare in the next recession (now projected for early 1989)? Although these larger carriers are flourishing now in the upturn and peak of the cycle, they will undoubtedly suffer some setbacks in any new recessionary period. Looking at the example of the two-tiered wage systems that were implemented by many carriers (including American) as a way of reducing costs, it will be noted that this system is based on growth. The only way average labour costs will drop is if the carrier experiences growth and as a result hires new employees on the lower tier of the system. As more and more new employees are hired, there is a corresponding drop in labour costs. What happens when the growth stops or when there is a net drop in market size, as in a recessionary phase? In this case the newer employees are laid off according to normal seniority rules and a situation ensues where labour costs are actually going up as a type 1 or reborn type 3 carrier goes into the downturn and pit of the next cycle. As the type 1s and reborn 3s are increasing their costs, the new entrant type 2s and 3s will be starting out with low costs, creating similar, although less drastic, conflicts and opportunities to the ones witnessed in the 1981–3 US recession. It seems clear that the inherent balance of power is a fluctuating one. The type 2s' and 3s' cost advantage is complemented during the downturn by changing consumer preferences. It is during these phases that the consumer is most likely preoccupied with low-cost travel on business or pleasure (see Fig. 2.16).

At this time in the cycle the type 2s and value-oriented type 3s have a very good opportunity to compete more effectively with the type 1s. In addition, the type 1s are also much less likely to commit diminishing funds to fighting the type 1s and 3s for small market

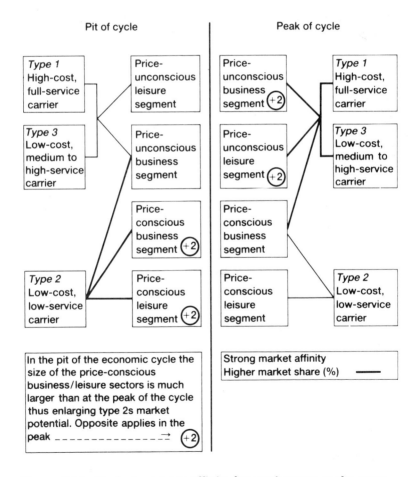

Figure 2.16 **Market segment affinity by carrier type at the extremities of the economic cycle**

shares. This allows the type 2s and 3s to build up market momentum and synergy. In sum, each carrier type has a preferred growth period; for type 1s and ex-type 1s it is during the upturn and the peak, while for the type 2s and 3s it is during the downturn and pit of the cycle.

The difficulty arises due to the fact that airlines, like people who run them, have short memories and tend to forget the lessons learnt during the last trip round the economic cycle.

When to consolidate

The term consolidation is usually not looked upon with favour in the aviation business, or any other business for that matter. It implies contraction, a reduction in revenues and profits and a series of sometimes painful cost-cutting exercises. Yet consolidations do occur, and different carrier types undertake them at different points in the economic cycle, whether willingly or not (Fig. 2.17). Some consolidations, such as Continental's use of Chapter 11, have proved successful; others have not. The key, as in identifying growth phases, is to recognize at which parts of the economic cycle consolidation should at least be contemplated. For People Express, the period from early 1985 until late 1988 would probably have been an ideal one for its consolidation. In opposition to the growth cycle, type 2s and type 3s should seek consolidation when the type 1s and ex-type 1s (now

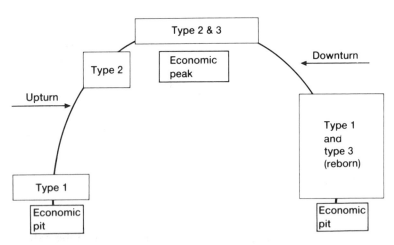

Figure 2.17 **Ideal phases for carrier consolidation**

type 3s) are at their strongest, during the upturn and peak. Type 1s and reborn type 3s tend to follow the normal economic trends by growing in the peaks and contracting in the downturn and pit of the cycle. For this reason it is easier for the established carriers to know when to contract since the market will often force them to do so regardless of their willingness to acquiesce. For the type 2 and original type 3, it is far more difficult to go contra-cycle even if the structural economic indicators show that this is a more prudent short-term strategy.

When to seek labour concessions

The management of the labour resource is critical to the success of any company but especially to those in the service industries like the airlines. Simply put, most companies seek to reduce costs when their performance is at its worst. For the type 1s and ex-type 1s, the ideal time would be during the downturn when employers in most industries are looking for and getting concessions. Figure 2.18 illustrates the ideal phases for obtaining labour concessions.

The last recession clearly showed that obtaining cost-reducing concessions was easiest at the pit of the recession when the alternative was usually lay offs or worse. At the pit of the cycle the new entrant type 2s and 3s were hiring new employees: People Express was hiring by the hundred. This shows that while the type 1s are

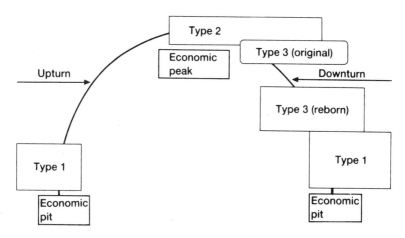

Figure 2.18 **Ideal phases for obtaining labour concessions**

reducing costs, usually in a slow and painful fashion, the type 2s and 3s are picking up trained staff for a fraction of the salary cost.

The difference between winners and losers within the type 1 and ex-type 1 category usually lies in the timing of contract negotiations. Some of the established type 1s and ex-type 1s were able to negotiate new deals just at or near the pit, thus achieving healthy cost reductions and more flexible job tasks which improve productivity. Those that through plain bad timing or other circumstances began negotiating as the economy turned around simply achieved fewer cost reductions. This discrepancy among the type 1 and ex-type 1 group helped some carriers do better than others. This labour cost advantage achieved in the pit stays with a carrier for the next cycle and thus helps it make even more money in the upturn and peak. The propensity towards strikes and other work disruptions is heightened during the upturn and peak when compared with negotiations that occur in the downturn and pit.

While the type 1s and ex-type 1s are able to negotiate their costs down in the downturn and pit, the type 2s and 3s do not. Often, as already discussed, the type 2s and 3s are increasing their staff size and achieving good growth during the downturn and pit. A second mechanism used by the type 2s and 3s has been a relatively low level of fixed income. At many of these new entrants the actual salary earned was only a fraction of total remuneration. Other components of the earnings package for employees included stock ownership plans and profit sharing. During the downturn and pit when type 2s and 3s are enjoying strong earnings in their stock value and their profits, employees can earn substantial windfalls if they perform well as a unit. Incentive tied earnings for employees have no doubt stimulated many to perform to a higher consistent standard and create pride in their company. Table 2.7 (opposite) compares productivity and cost for 1986. (See also Fig. 2.7)

The big problem for type 2s and 3s comes when the economy turns around. At that point the bigger type 1s and ex-type 1s are gaining strength and making money again. They are hiring or at least recalling laid off employees, thus drying up the pool of ready-trained labour on which the type 2s and 3s had been drawing. In order to be competitive in their hiring, the type 2s and 3s now have to pay the going rate for new employees, if they are in a position to hire any. To add to their woes, as their financial performance declines due to heavier competition and a switch away from 'price only' consumer segments, the profit-sharing and appreciating stock ownership plans that their employees had invested in begin to decline. All of a sudden

Table 2.7 Productivity and Cost comparisons for US carriers for the year 1986

	AA	CO	DL	EA	NW	PA	TW	UA	AL	PI
Revenue* ($)	5.85	2.01	4.51	4.40	3.59	3.04	3.14	7.10	1.78	1.7
Operating Expenses* ($)	5.46	1.87	4.28	4.33	3.42	3.33	3.22	7.03	1.62	1.6
Operating Profit† ($)	392	143	230	65	166	(−293)	(−575)	73	164	153
Wages as % of expenses	37.6	24.5	46.2	39.4	30.1	37.5	35.4	36.4	41.7	35.2
Fuel as % of expenses	16	19.4	14.2	16.4	18.6	14.9	16.3	15.6	14.4	14.7
Wages as % of cost per ASM‡	38.3	22.4	45.6	38.2	28.9	33.2	36.2	36.1	42.1	34
Yield (cents)	10.2	8.66	13.2	11.41	10.1	10.2	9.66	10	14.93	15.8
Revenue/employee ($)	113.2	105.3	115.8	105.8	107.4	140.7	114.6	120.4	119.3	89.2
Operating profit/employee ($)	7.5	7.49	5.9	1.5	4.9	(-13.5)	(-2.7)	1.24	10.9	7.8
Employees/aircraft	157	91	151	145	107	189	133	162	101	122

*Billions of US dollars.
† Millions of US dollars.
‡ ASM = Average seat mile.
AA: American; Co: Continental; DL: Delta; EA: Eastern;
NW: Northwest: PA: Pan AM; PI: Piedmont; TW: TWA:
UA: United: AL: US Air.
Source: Airline Executive, June 1987.

the flexible remuneration scheme that had seemed so attractive to employees of type 2 and type 3 carriers in the good times (the downturn and pit of the cycle), does not seem so valuable anymore. Before long, the employees at type 2 and type 3 carriers are asking for basic wages and there begins to be a threat of unionization. This particular phenomenon was illustrated by the unionization by ALPA of the Midway pilots and the continuous threat of unionization at People Express. As if all of these issues were not enough for the previously low-cost type 2s and 3s, the fact remains that the time to ask for concessions is in times of worst economic performance for the carrier group. The time for consolidation for the type 2s and 3s is during the upturn and peak. Just when all of the type 2 and type 3 carrier employee groups are seeing their neighbours and friends from other sectors beginning to enjoy the fruits of the general economic revival that follows the recessionary phase, they find out they have to tighten their belts. This contra-normal trend for type 2s and type 3s is very difficult to justify to employees despite the fact that it is the outcome of a very real economic phenomenon.

The fact remains that if the type 2s and 3s ignore this chance for cost reduction they risk being less competitive in the next downturn and being more vulnerable to attack from new type 2s or 3s which will enter the market with lower costs in the next downturn.

The offsetting benefit for the type 2s and 3s is that most of them are not unionized. Therefore by replacing fixed and regular increases with incentives, they may be able to convince employees of the longer-term benefits of making concessions despite the poor performance of the stock or profit-sharing plan in the upturn and peak of the cycle. It is clear that remuneration based on the incentive performance mechanism is designed to reward only when corporate performance allows. The problem is explaining this fact to employees who see peak economic activity in other industry sectors around them. It is clear, however, that the type 2s and 3s that are successful in limiting their labour cost increases in the upturn of the ecomony will carry a decided cost advantage over both type 1s and other type 2s and 3s who have not been successful in doing so.

When to buy aircraft

This particular component tends to follow a more traditional expectation. The ideal time to buy aircraft for any type of carrier is a short time before the upturn and peak for that airline type (See Fig. 2.19). For type 1s and ex-type 1s the ideal time is just after the pit in the early upturn of the cycle. Ordering aircraft then means that deliveries will have been made just before peak utilization (due to high market growth) begins. For the type 2s and 3s the ideal time is just before their peak growth periods which happen to be in the downturn and pit of the cycle. For type 2s and 3s this buying timing applies to both new aircraft and used ones. It is clear that used aircraft come onto the market rather quickly as the path of the economic downturn steepens. Therefore the type 2s and 3s are more or less conditioned by the lowering of prices and complementary increase in availability of used aircraft. As for new aircraft, the price of these also tends to come down as the economy turns sour. The interesting caveat to these cyclical ebbs and flows of the aircraft market is the significant advent of mega-leasing companies. The question becomes whether these leasing companies will influence the traditional methods and timing of aircraft disposal in the downturn. It could be that type 2s and 3s will not wish to lease encumbered aircraft in a recession when they can buy used ones outright from other carriers.

By the same token, will type 1 and ex-type 1 carriers who are considering letting capacity go decide to turn back leased-in aircraft in favour of ones they own? The impact of high interest rates on capital equipment intensive balance sheets is significant. It may be cheaper to keep older, wholly-owned aircraft and turn back leased ones. It may even become a deliberate strategy by the type 1s and ex-type 1s to reduce the flow of used aircraft to their type 2 and 3 brethren. Since the next economic recession will be the first where the real mega-sized leasing companies will participate, it remains to be seen what the actual impact will be. It seems likely, however, that despite potential reductions in the flows of used aircraft on the market, many type 2s and 3s will find the equipment they need at relatively cheap prices in the downturn and pit of the cycle.

The key point is that carriers, no matter what type, rarely take delivery of aircraft at the right time. Type 1s and ex-type 1s usually buy aircraft when they feel thay can afford them and this is usually on the upturn or the actual peak of the cycle. The actual deliveries tend to be sometime later, often during the downturn and pit of the cycle. As such, the type 1s and ex-type 1s take delivery of new capacity and debt when they can least afford them. So, in the normal course of

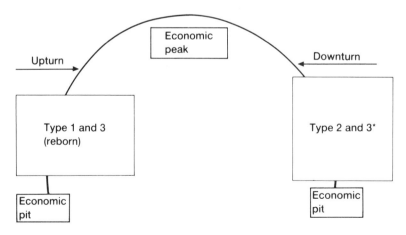

* Includes second-hand aircraft

Figure 2.19 **Ideal phase for fleet purchase**

events, the type 1s and ex-type 1s must go against their usual tendency when acquiring aircraft. For the type 2 and 3 airlines, things are a bit easier. They take on used aircraft when they need them, which just happens to coincide with a lowering of price and an increase of supply of used planes. Similarly, the prices for new aircraft have usually come down by the mid-downturn phase of the recessionary slide. As such, type 2s and 3s who are growing in the downturn can take on new aircraft at lower costs as well. The net result is that the type 2s and 3s would seem to have an easier and more advantageous timing for acquiring aircraft, either used or new. Three supplementary factors could affect the pattern of aircraft movement in the next recession: (1) a healthy increase in fuel prices (2) the implementation of more stringent noise criteria thus rendering many otherwise good second-hand aircraft unusable and (3) the improved cost efficiency of type 1s and ex-type 1s when compared to the last recession. The third issue would simply serve to reduce the fleet size decrease required by the incumbent carriers in the next recessionary phase and thus reduce the number of second-hand aircraft coming onto the market.

The countervailing effect could be imposed by significantly higher fuel prices. If this were to occur at or just after the next economic peak, then the established carriers could order many newer, more fuel-efficient types and thus start dumping older, less efficient types onto the second-hand market. This would, of course, serve to enhance supply, thus dropping the price for second-hand aircraft and facilitating type 2 and 3 fleet acquisition plans. The optimization of fleet purchase timing will remain a key critical element in overall carrier success no matter what the airline type. The essential factor that must be recognized is that each type of carrier has a different optimal fleet acquisition timing that is more dificult for type 1 and ex-type 1 carriers to apply than new entrant and existing type 2s and 3s.

The issue of seeking more investment capital

The need for additional capital is continuous in a capital-intensive industry such as air transportation. It is true that every type of carrier can seek capital at most times despite the fact that Wall Street seems to try to play the winners whenever it can. Bearing in mind the different natural growth periods for the various types of carrier, one could assume that type 1s and ex-type 1s have an easier time obtaining investment capital during the upturn and peak while the type 2s and 3s are the opposite. To a certain extent this is true. If it is assumed that the market and venture capitalists have a finite amount of capital to expend in a given period and that in the downturn and pit the new entrant type 2s and 3s are using up a higher proportion of that investment power, then the type 1s and ex-type 1s will have less for themselves. Also true is the fact that in a recession the type 1s and ex-type 1s are invariably in a recessive consolidation mode which requires less capital. In fact, the reduction of costs and liquidation of assets that are saleable tend to reduce their need for cash. Consequently the markets that will seek to invest in the best places possible turn to the carriers that are expanding rapidly and require cash infusions to fuel growth, and these are invariably the type 2s and 3s in the downturn of the economic cycle.

The absolute amount of funding required by the new entrants tends to be smaller than that needed by the big established type 1s and ex-type 1s, thus having a smaller impact on available investment funds and certainly leaving some market capacity for the type 1s and ex-type 1s even in a recession. The thing that helps the better established and better performing ex-type 1s such as Northwest and Delta are their good long-term financial track records. This confidence tends to allow easier access to funds for them than, say, an Eastern Airlines might have enjoyed in the last recession. The reduction in need for funds by the bigger type 1s and ex-type 1s in a recession does open the door for easier funds access to existing type 2s and 3s as well as to

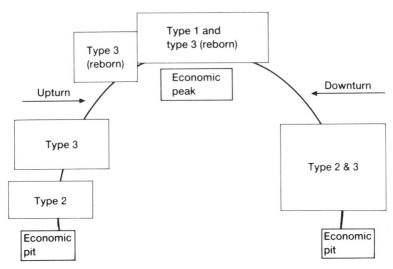

Figure 2.20 Availability of investment capital (indicates primary flows of capital)

aspiring new entrants looking to float their initial stock offerings. Another thing that helps the type 2s and 3s is their contra-normal economic growth periods. While companies in many sectors tend to be down and losing money, the type 2 and 3 airlines are some of the few companies that are growing and generating cash and profits. This tends to make the question of who to invest in much easier. After all, many people must travel even during a recession, but they will usually do it at lower fares and be willing to accept a lower standard. This type of transport usually tends to be better done by the type 2 and 3 carriers.

Overall, therefore, the general rule of thumb is that the funding to fuel expansion is most readily obtainable for the type 1s and ex-type 1s which are now 3s in the upturn and peak of the cycle while for the type 2s and 3s it is more readily available at the pit and early upturn (see Fig. 2.20).

The overall strategic approach

The foregoing section has indicated that all the factors of production tend to support very different strategies for the various types of carrier. The optimal overall strategy for each type is obtained by combining the sub-strategies and building an overall generic corporate strategy. All of these strategies are governed by the sometimes harsh realities of the economic cycle.

The fact that deregulation has removed the protective cocoon that once enveloped the industry means that carriers must now face the world on their own like companies in any other industry. As in any other service industry with high barriers to entry, the tendency towards an oligopolistic structure seems inevitable. This does not mean to say that innovation will not enter the marketplace in the person of new entrant type 2 or 3 carriers. In fact, as previously discussed, the number of new entrants may drop but the flow will not be extinguished as long as the open unregulated market philosophy persists.

What does the future hold?

If history and the experience of the first go around the economic cycle under a deregulated regime in the US are any indication, then turbulent would probably be as good a word as any to describe the future.

Many analysts have taken the view that the so-called shake-out phase of the US domestic air transport industry is over. Most of the mergers are over and the remaining giants can sustain themselves on their own. After all, now that they have achieved gargantuan size they have become immune to the rigours of the economic cycle, right? Some of the biggest carriers in 1980 felt the effects of deregulation the most. Those that tried to swallow up competitors in the early 1980s are either no longer in existence or in severe financial peril. Why should another tour around the economic cycle be any different? The only key difference is that all of the surviving carriers have already been through one cycle and trimmed down their costs accordingly. Those costs have begun to creep up, however, and the coming recession will again force them to cut costs and consolidate. Depending on how much one believes the stock market crash of 1987 will affect world economic cycles, the projections for the next recession are for early to mid 1989. The actual date is of less importance than the fact that we know that sooner or later there will be another recession and it will eventually be followed by a recovery. What impacts will this have on the air transport industry in the next 1–3 years?

The era of the new entrants – Act 2

There is one key factor that will determine how many new entrants come into the market over the next 12–36 months and that is the actual level of decline shown by the economic GNP curve in the US. The last recession dipped below the −2 GNP growth level thus setting off a trend of great dislocation and subsequent consolidation. By the same token, this drop in economic production also helped set off the influx of many dozens of new entrant carriers into the marketplace. As we now know, few of these survived the upturn and only one managed to achieve significant market size and synergy.

It seems normal to assume that once again in the next recession big carriers will lose money, trim costs, dump excess aircraft and non-profitable routes, lay off trained employees, sell off terminal gates and slots, offer idle maintenance capacity to new entrants at low rates, etc. At what point will the financial life-blood start to haemorrhage from the bigger carriers? Invariably these periods of big carrier haemorrhage serve as transfusions into the new entrants. The downturn of the economic cycle seems to help the new entrants permeate the market. A qualifying criterion would be that since the bigger carriers are veterans of one deregulated recession their panic point will be a little later into the recession than it was last time. So expect fewer new entrants than last time, but expect more than a couple. The actual flow of new entrants will be, as previously stated, regulated by the severity of the downturn. A −3 GNP rate would really do wonders for the new entrants although nothing so drastic as a depression is recommended for any carrier.

What kind of carrier will these new entrants be? It seems likely that a majority will try to become type 2s. Any carrier born in 1988 or 1989 will have lower costs starting out than any of the existing type 2s let alone the type 1s and 3s. Since a recession brings out the frugal aspect of most individuals and corporations, the low-cost, low-service carrier will be back in vogue. The difference this time will be that there will be no significant influx of dormant air travel demand since most of these passengers flew during the last recession.

Since the dormant, untapped market is much smaller, it leaves the conversion of passengers from road and railways to air travel as the sole significant additional source of market growth. The rate of this conversion will depend on a variety of factors, including the escalation of fuel prices and the decrease of gross disposable income in the next recession. The worse the scenario for consumers the more people will leave their ageing cars at home and travel for $19 or $29 each way on the newest of new entrants in 1989, Son of People Express Inc. It could even be run by the original People Express President Don Burr who has no specific air carrier affiliation that could not be broken. This new airline would survive on building itself a hub at the next underutilized airport in the New York area, Stewart Field, and charging lower than low fares to all of the most popular destinations where the lowest prevailing fares are still relatively high. Sound familiar? It seems likely that the industry life-cycle has left itself open to this kind of carrier once again. The existing type 2s will have a hard time defending against this type of carrier since the new entrant's cost structure will be lower than theirs. The new entrant type 2s will be able to charge the lowest fare and still make money by having lower costs, using second-hand aircraft, non-unionized labour employed on flexible job tasks, and new hub airports in close proximity to major centres (although many of these are now used up). There will also be some new entrants that will try their luck at being type 3 carriers by using the low-cost base of a new entrant and a medium to full-service differentiated type of product. This segment will be more difficult to penetrate than the last time around because some of the larger well-established carriers are starting the downturn as a type 3, in contrast to 1980–2 when all established carriers started as type 1s. Carriers at the top end of the market did not have much success last time around and their fate would seem similarly tinted this time around due primarily to the fact that the established full-service carriers are healthier than last time. Figure 2.21 shows the evolution of US carriers between 1978 and 1990.

Around the cycle again for the familiar players

And what of the big type 1A, type 2A and type 3A carriers? Who will thrive, who will survive and who will perish?

Specific issues are certain to influence this group, not the least of which are costs of operation. A sample of the coming problems for incumbent carriers of all types could include the following. Starting with the newest big carrier, it would appear that carriers such as Texas Air Corp., who are still trying to digest all of their acquisitions, are vulnerable. In the recession, interest rates will go up, thereby making the $3.9 billion of debt that Texas Air owns very difficult to live with. The amalgamation of the various labour groups at Eastern with those of other Texas Air carriers seems a difficult and time-consuming task. If Continental does not manage to trim debt, consolidate its workforce and avoid major additional infrastructural fixed costs they will have lost the sole advantage that may allow them to survive the next recessionary phase, namely type 2A low-cost operating structure. Interestingly, Continental is spending heavily to try and repair its tattered consumer service image. This is, of course, a valid strategy in a period of economic growth, but if Continental is not able to shed these costs by the time the downturn starts in earnest they may lose out altogether.

American has been a prolific practitioner of the independent growth strategy with the exception of their purchase of Air Cal which, according to Mr Crandall, was not a departure from AA's avowed independent growth strategy but simply the filling of a regional void in their network. As can be seen from Table 2.8, AA has expanded the size of its operation from 40 134 000 passengers in 1978 to 51 095 000 (incl. Air Cal) in 1986; the employee growth was from 40 134 in 1978 to 51 100 (incl. Air Cal) in 1986 with passengers handled per employee going from 697 in 1978 to 1000 (incl. Air Cal) in 1986. That made American bigger than any US carrier except Delta and Continental (incl. Eastern) in terms of passengers carried in 1986; it was the fourth largest passenger carrier in 1978. The fact

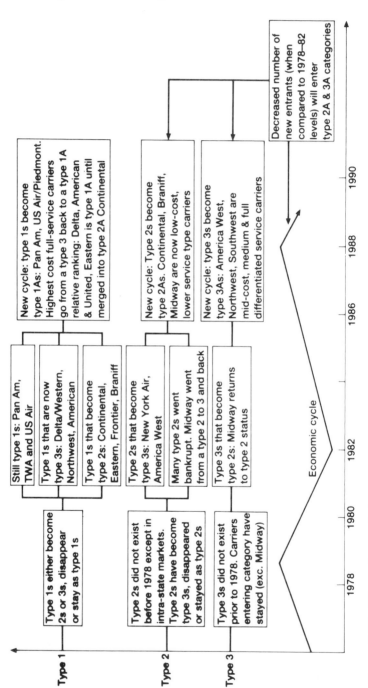

Figure 2.21 US carrier evolution 1978–90

that American has grown so much from within is a key part of the rationale behind their two-tier wage scale. The more growth, the more employees and the lower the average wage rate and labour cost. Between 1983 and 1986, American added 10 974 employees (not including Air Cal) and most of these came in at the second of the two-tiered wage scales. The issue with this system, as mentioned in a previous section, for American and all carriers with two-tiered wage systems is that in the next recession these lower cost human resources could be laid off. This realization has prompted review of this policy at American.

As this occurs, using the standard seniority provisions, American and other carriers in a similar situation will watch market growths

Table 2.8 Comparison of largest US carriers

	United	American	Delta	Northwest	Piedmont	US Air	Pan Am	†TWA
1978								
Employees	50 807	40 134	32 281	8 036	3 446	8 459	26 964	36 250
Passengers (000)	40 729	27 989	36 256	6 575	4 580	12 838	8 675	19 276
Passengers/ Employee	802	697	1 123	818	1 329	1 518	322	544
1986								
Employees	54 824*	47 898	37 312	33 296	15 297	14 520	26 117	31 698
Passengers (000)	50 480*	46 071	41 038	20 439	22 796	21 725	12 466	20 042
Passengers/ employee	921*	962	1 100	614	1 490	1 496	477	632

1986 figures plus subsidiary carriers	+Air Cal	+Western	+Republic		Piedmont		+Ozark
Employees	51 100	48 828	47 356		29 817		35 834
Passengers (000)	51 095	53 272	37 881		44 521		25 583
Passengers/ employee	1 000	1 091	800		1 493		714

* Numbers include Pan Am Pacific network.
† Pan Am figures include National Airlines but exclude Pan Am Pacific network.

drop due to the recession, labour costs rise and profits drop. While these laid-off employees find work at new entrant carriers at lower wages than the second-tier wages at American and other carriers, the established carriers will be watching their costs go up thus increasing the cost gap between type 1s and new entrant type 2s and 3s. The only interim solution seems to be the obtaining of more flexible job tasks which would improve productivity among all employees thus off-setting the rising costs engendered by the laying off of the second tier of the two-tier scale. In addition, as CRS competition escalates, American will have less of a financial cross-subsidy facility from Sabre (as Sabre profits erode).

Looking at some specific carriers and their likely activities in the next cycle, the following is noted. Eastern is no longer an individual carrier and thus can be removed from the endangered list. The two other carriers that have been having a difficult time of it include TWA and Pan Am. TWA helped itself by buying Ozark, thus consolidating its St Louis hub and raising its passengers carried from 19 726 000 in 1978 to 25 583 000 in 1986. The key attribute of the TWA/Ozark merger was the acquisition of a stronger domestic traffic feed system for TWA international flights. The fact remains, however, that TWA

Merger deals have become prevalent in many US
industries although US airlines have had their
fair share of big deals in 1986. Airline mergers as compared to
all US mergers rank as follows:

25   United purchases Hilton International – $980 million

50   Delta purchases Western – $651 million

57   Texas Air purchases Eastern Airlines – $605 million

74   Northwest purchases Republic – $550 million

103 Northwest purchases 50% of Pars from TWA – $400 million

182 Texas Air purchases People Express – $229 million

186 TWA purchases Ozark – $224 million

Figure 2.22 **Merger mania during the upturn and peak of the economic cycle**
Source: Business Week, 1986

had a net combined loss of –$281 908 000 between 1983 and 1986. The Chernobyl and terrorism-filled summer of 1986 did not help the still internationally dependent carrier. The fact that many stronger US domestic carriers have now developed strong international networks hasn't helped TWA. While TWA will probably have a good 1987, so will virtually every other carrier. The pent-up demand from the previous year has made any carrier with aircraft look relatively good in 1987. With heightened international competition from stronger international carriers, the trend towards international carrier consolidation and an impending US domestic recession, the future does not bode well for carriers that are already strained to the limit. One could see a major alliance on the international front for TWA in the next 2–3 years or even a consolidation with another US carrier seeking a quick fix to international transatlantic growth (United?).

As difficult as things seem at TWA, one would have to conclude that things are worse at Pan Am. Constant rumours of takeover by outside companies, an ageing fleet, the terrible summer of 1986, some of the highest labour costs in the industry, the damaging acquisition of National, the lack of significant domestic network, heightened international competition from other US carriers and foreign international carriers, the list goes on and on. A combined loss of –$469 328 000 between 1983–6 did not help matters either. The corporate strategy has forcibly had to be one of asset stripping to stay alive. From buildings to aircraft, to their Pacific route network, to hotels and now Board approval to sell off most of the rest of Pan Am's assets: one wonders where it will all end. Pan Am now rivals Continental and several Third World nations in terms of long-term debt and things show little sign of improvement. The only things of value left at Pan Am are the Atlantic and intra-European route licences that it holds. Passengers handled per employee at Pan Am went from 322 in 1978 to an industry worst 477 in 1986 which was 1016 fewer passengers per employee than 1986 industry leader US Air/Piedmont at 1493. One wonders how long it will go on and most prognostications would not see Pan Am surviving the next recession in its present form. Liquidation of Pan Am and redistribution of its route rights could be the most efficient solution although many creditors would be left holding a rather large debt with little hope of recovering it through asset sale. The departure of Pan Am could clear the way for a new entrant international carrier although it would be more logical to assume another established type 1A carrier will fill the breach.

Sub-strategies in the next recession.

Some differences between the last recessionary cycle and this one will revolve around network development. Last time many cities such as Newark, Kansas City, Phoenix, Raleigh-Durham, Dayton, Cincinnati, Cleveland, Midway Airport (Chicago), Dulles Airport (Washington), Salt Lake City and many others did not have hub or mini-hub operations headquartered there. In addition, several other hubs such as Charlotte, Baltimore/Washington and others were not as well developed second-generation hubs as they are today. The issue becomes finding a market slot for the new entrant to key on.

A subsidiary issue is one which deals with the question of how many carriers will be able to maintain strength at multiple hubs? Will Continental be able to maintain Newark, Miami, Houston and keep up in the constant fight with United for dominance at Denver? Will the new US Air/Piedmont manage to keep all of their hubs at Pittsburgh, Philadelphia, Dayton, Charlotte, Baltimore and Syracuse competitive? The ability to maintain market strength and dominance at multiple hubs will be a new skill for many carriers and one which may not be easy to practise. Every hub is prone to attack, especially by low-fare type 2 new entrants, and the incumbent carrier will have to decide how much money they will expend to defend a hub and which hubs in order of priority they would be most willing to defend. Of the fifty US airports with passengers over 500 000 (second quarter 1987), fifteen showed the leading carrier with in excess of 45 per cent of the total; another eighteen show the number one carrier with in excess of 25 per cent of the airport total; of the seventeen remaining airports, San Diego, Orlando, Los Angeles, Las Vegas, Columbus and Boston are key undefended hubs (data from *Aviation Daily*, Nov. 1987). Airports like Los Angeles and Boston are difficult to penetrate because of slot constraints at key times but the others could represent a home base for new entrants. It is in fact true that infrastructural constraints at key airports help the incumbent hub carrier in any hub war unless the government opts to legislate more equal access to slots and gates at that airport, as has been done in the past. Another way for a new entrant to install itself could be to buy out one of the smaller existing type 2 or type 3 carriers and build a base at the acquired hub. Finally, one must wonder when the US market will have reached saturation point on the number of hubs within its borders. While Columbus remains one of the few unexploited hubs of any magnitude, it is doubtful whether the state of Ohio can withstand a fourth hub (after Cincinnati, Dayton, Cleveland) within its borders. There can be no doubt that there will be fewer new hubs established this time around the economic cycle but that more inter-hub rivalry will develop with the quality of hubs and the transit experience they offer consumers taking on a new importance. Hub wars will become commonplace with the losers abandoning hubs instead of losing their whole airline to the competition.

With no or negative growth it stands to reason that in the recessionary phase some hubs will change hands and two to four newer ones will be created. Several analysts also predict a return to more of a linear network which overflies hubs. This revised network strategy may eventually come about simply because it is different from the *status quo* or because it does offer customers more direct access to key points. The chances of this change happening during a recession are limited simply because linear-type networks are much more expensive to operate than hubs and in a recession that kind of additional expense may be difficult to sustain.

Strategic snapshot: airline advertising.

Airline advertising serves not only to highlight those facts that carriers wish the travelling public to become more conscious of, but also as a method of deciphering which areas are the most hotly competitive between airlines at any given time. At the peak of the US domestic economic cycle we know that consumers and therefore the airlines place a far greater emphasis on product quality and features and less on price-only criteria. During the fall of 1987, US carriers were placing a great emphasis on product quality. The largest carrier, Continental, was being attacked by the other major US carriers for its poor service and unreliable product quality. While a portion of that assertion was justified, it became clear that the major carriers also had an ulterior motive in mind. The major carriers were clearly jealous of Continental's very low cost/ seat mile which American classified as 'obscene'. The majors said that with such a low cost structure Continental could not deliver the product it had promised. It is for that reason that American began to champion causes such as a minimum industry wage level, which would raise Continental's closer to that of the other major carriers. The majors also lobbied for public reporting of on-time performance and other product performance criteria, all of which was designed to show up Continental's defective product. The theory on the part of the majors was that if they put on enough pressure, Continental would be forced to increase its cost of operation by hiring more people and investing more in providing better service quality. This would in turn help the majors close the cost gap between themselves and Continental before the next recession when price will once again return as the prime consumer carrier selection criteria. The carrier with the lowest costs will, of course, be able to profitably charge the lowest fare. The following advertisements show a direct confrontation between American, with its 'flying garbage can campaign' and an advertisement which appeared in the form of an open letter from Continental Chairman, Frank Lorenzo to the public. The Continental advertisement, which appeared in a variety of publications was entitled 'Once people called us The Proud Bird. Lately they've been calling us other names', and was followed by this text:

'Continental is no stranger to success. As "The Proud Bird", passengers were calling weeks in advance to be sure of getting a seat with us. But recently, while we combined the operations of four airlines, we grew so fast that we made mistakes. Misplaced baggage. Delays. Reservation errors. You were frustrated and angry. And a lot of hardworking people at Continental were pretty embarrassed.

'It's led to an intensified commitment to quality. And it's beginning to pay off. Latest reports show Continental's back as one of the top two airlines in on-time arrivals. But we're out to be "America's Best". To get there, we're investing more than $1.25 billion this year alone (*advertisement appeared in 1987*) to upgrade airport facilities and aircraft and to expand our fleet.

'We're continually evaluating and adjusting our flight schedules for better connections and on-time performance. Working to decrease lost baggage – an area where we've already improved 100% in the last six months. Even adding special trouble-shooters at major airports who can respond instantly if problems occur. But that's just the start.

We think we'll be the talk of the airline industry. And believe me, it won't sound anything like what you've been hearing lately.' *signed Frank Lorenzo*

Other carriers including TWA, Pan Am, Northwest and Delta are all using service as a key theme in their advertising. Even in Europe we note that most carriers are using their advertising to talk about things like mechanical and schedule reliability, the virtues of their resident hubs and the width and breadth of their route network and new service products. As previously discussed, in the upturn and peak of the economic cycle the primary emphasis of most advertising shifts to follow key consumer preferences. The confrontation between a type 2 (Continental) and type 1 to 3 carriers makes for interesting, competitive advertising that is different from the usual (strictly price oriented) advertising we saw so much of during the 1981–83 period (recessionary phase) in the US.

Pages 97 - 101 reproduced by courtesy of American Airlines
Pages 102 - 104 reproduced by courtesy of Piedmont Airlines

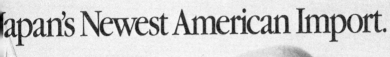

Japan's Newest American Import.

arting May 21, American Airlines introduces service to Tokyo.

May 21, American Airlines l be able to treat your cli- s to something very special. r new nonstops from Dallas/ t Worth to Tokyo's Narita port, with convenient con- tions from cities through- the East, Southwest and lwest.

e roomiest seating to e Far East.

With American's International Flagship Service[SM]

and our specially designed 747SP, we offer more pas- senger space to Tokyo than any other airline. Includ- ing plush sleeper seats in First Class. Spa- cious 6-across seating in Business Class. Separate stand-up bars for the added relax- ation of both your First Class and Business Class clients. And, in Economy Class, complimentary beverage service and sushi appetizers.

More special services.

We'll also pamper your clients with plenty of extras, like first-run inflight movies. Free stereo head- sets. Extra-large storage bins, providing more room for carry- on luggage. And a choice of excellent Japanese or American cuisine.

Miles that really add up.

Your clients can even earn dou- ble mileage credit in American's AAdvantage® travel awards pro- gram, based on class of service flown, when flying from the Dallas/Fort Worth gateway to Tokyo through July 31, 1987. And their

miles can add up to earn travel awards including First Class upgrades and free trips to other exciting American Airlines destinations: Hawaii, Mexico, the Caribbean, Europe and more.

When you have clients bound for Japan, book American. And let us treat them to the comfort of Japan's newest American import.

Schedules subject to change without notice. AAdvantage® is a registered service mark of American Airlines, Inc. AAdvantage program rules, regulations, travel awards and special offers are subject to change without notice and subject to any applicable foreign laws.

AmericanAirlines
Something special to Japan.

DoMechani
You StuckOi

T*hese days we hear more and more about flights delayed or cancelled for mechanical reasons. Are the airlines doing a poor job of maintaining their planes?*

At American Airlines, we've substantially reduced both mechanical delays and cancellations.

We've done it by committing ourselves to the very best maintenance program we know how to create. Day in. Day out.

We spend over $1.8 million a day on maintenance.

In total, we spend more than $650 million a year on maintenance—an average of well over $1.5 million per year per plane.

But money is only part of the story. We field over 7,500 highly trained employees dedicated solely to maintenance excellence.

These people plan and execute maintenance programs that far exceed government requirements. We set our own high standards. And we stick to them.

It all begins with major maintenance.

Every plane in our fleet receives major maintenance at precise intervals. And when we say major maintenance, we mean it. Every system is meticulously checked. And rechecked. Everything from avionics computers to landing gear.

We give the airframe a detailed structural inspection and the engines an inside look.

And we don't just look, either. We bring all the technology we can find to bear. For example, we x-ray more than 5,000 parts every year and use a wide range of equipment—like borescopes and ultrasonic instruments—to test what we can't see. And when nothing else satisfies us, we simply take it all apart.

No plane goes back into service until everything is shipshape. Inside and out. Top to bottom. From one end to the other.

And we don't let up for a minute.

Between major maintenance visits, we do a whole series of special checks—from daily once-overs to very heavy checks at longer intervals.

And of course, any malfunction whatsoever—from an oil consumption rate that's a pint per hour too high to an instrument panel light that blinks—is recorded in the logbook and then in our computerized tracking system.

Our computers track the maintenance history of every one of our 396 planes.

So we know exactly what needs to be done. What's been done. When it was done. And who did it.

Right down to every nut and bolt.

And when all that checking tells us a new part is needed, the same computer system gets it to the right place at the right time—along with a message about the right way to use it.

So whatever needs fixing is fixed—as fast as our people and resources can get it done right.

We're committed to mechanical excellence.

In fact, our mechanics spend 12 hours working on a plane for every hour it flies.

Despite all this effort, we can't say that mechanical delays will never happen on American Airlines because if there's even the smallest malfunction, we won't take off until it's checked out.

Our goal is better and better maintenance to reduce, even further, the things that need a last-minute check.

And it's working. We've had fewer maintenance delays this year than last, and next year we'll be better still.

We know your schedule is important—and we're doing all we can to make our reliability the standard for the world.

Number three in a series devoted to issues facing the flying public.

AmericanAirlines
Something special in the air.®

l Delays Have
he Ground?

If The Plane Is A
That Tell You A

Today, some airlines seem more interested in filling planes than cleaning them. In an effort to cut costs, some carriers have cut way back on services.

American doesn't want you to think that all airlines ignore the demands of their customers.

That's why we'd like to address just one of the many steps we take to help assure passenger comfort.

We work hard to keep our fleet clean.

Every year, we spend over $30 million cleaning our planes.

Our 72-point cleaning checklist helps us deliver the quality you've come to expect from American.

Every day we pick up, wash, wipe, scrub, scour, dust, polish, sanitize, refresh, replenish, replace, disinfect, arrange and rearrange our 389 American airplanes.

And that commitment to cleanliness doesn't stop with our interiors.

Next time you see one of our aircraft, take a look at our silver exteriors. That shine on our face is not achieved with a once-over-lightly washing.

We do it all by hand. Even the polishing. Hand-held buffers go over every square inch of our planes. Imagine waxing over 100 cars and you have some idea of the magnitude of polishing just one of our planes.

American is committed to doing the job right. Not just sometimes. But all the time.

That's not to say that on occasion, when we turn a plane fast to make an on-time departure, we won't miss a spot or fail to clean an ashtray or overlook a scrap of paper in the seat pocket. But rest assured, these oversights will be corrected before the day is out.

Dedicated to superior service.

Cost cutting will never come before cleanliness at American Airlines. Keeping our planes clean is a reflection of an attitude that runs through our entire organization. We are dedicated to giving you superior service on every flight because we know it's something our passengers expect from us.

To be successful, we must continue to deliver a better way to fly. That's the American Way.

Number two in a series devoted to issues facing the flying public.

AmericanAirlines
Something special in the air.

ess,What Does ut The Airline?

The Airline Th
Been Rated Hig
Service With
Even Having Firs
Introduces First

In a survey of frequent flyers that was conducted by the travel newsletter

Andrew Harper's Hideaway Report, Piedmont Airlines beat every other major

airline in America. And we did it with what

amounts to one hand tied behind our back.

That hand is now untied.

Because we've just introduced first class service as superior to the industry's standard as our coach service has

traditionally been.

The superiority be

with the price. For ju
$20 to $60 each way

First Class. For As Little As $20

's
st In
t
lass,
lass.

regular coach fares,
dmont is offering a fully
firmed first class seat.

And unlike most
nes, Piedmont doesn't
ke you forfeit valuable
quent flyer bonus miles,
ettle for "standby" first
s status.
et despite our low
s, what we're offering
rst class amounts to
hing less than an
barrassment of riches.

r Coach.♦

Not just gourmet
cuisine served to you on
fine china atop linen.
Not just a complimentary
newspaper. On longer

flights, you can expect
truly luxurious amenities
of a sort seldom seen

anymore in air travel.
Such as a fresh flower

in a crystal vase. And wine
that is uncorked for your

approval at your seat.
In addition, you'll enjoy

separate check-in facilities
at many airports. Flight
attendants who will store
your carry-on luggage for
you. And the luxury of
having your checked

luggage loaded last so it
comes off the plane first.
What's more, our first
class will be available on
every Piedmont jet, from
our widebody 767's to our
Fokker F-28's.
So call Piedmont or
your travel agent to make
reservations.
Because if you're one
of those who thought our
coach service was first
class, you'll be groping for
new adjectives to describe
our first class ╱ service.

PIEDMONT
A Model Of How Good
An Airline Can Be.

© Piedmont Airlines, 1987

Now You Don't Have To Be Rich And Famous To Fly First Class.

At last, there's a first class you can afford even if you didn't just sign a five-picture deal with Warner Brothers.

On Piedmont Airlines, you can get a fully confirmed first class seat for just $20 to $60 each way over our regular coach fares.

Yet you'll enjoy amenities of a sort seldom found in air travel today.

Such as a fresh flower in a crystal vase. Wine that is actually uncorked at your seat. Separate check-in facilities at many airports. And the luxury of having your checked luggage loaded last so it comes off the plane first.

What's more, with our extra-wide seats, you'll never be forced to rub elbows with any beautiful people who may be seated next to you.

So call Piedmont or your travel agent. And experience firsthand, the lifestyles of the rich and famous.

PIEDMONT

First Class. As Low As $20 Over Coach.

Prices vary according to destination and do not apply to transatlantic service.

©Piedmont Airlines, 1987

Key marketing objectives

As is customary in other industries, the key marketing objectives change to reflect consumers' tastes, even if the marketing response lags actual consumer taste changes. In the upturn/peak, customer service, amenities and other related items are key variables. The current fight between American, Delta, Northwest, United and Continental illustrates this point very well. All of the old line carriers such as Delta and American are making thinly-veiled remarks about Continental's less than adequate customer service levels. At the same time the October 1987 customer complaint records (see Table 2.9) (carriers are now forced to file these monthly with the government) showed that Northwest had the worst record of all with 634 passenger complaints versus Continental's 613. One of the other Texas Air carriers, Eastern, was third worst with 517 complaints. Piedmont was best among larger carriers with 73 complaints. Interestingly, when it came to on-time performance, Continental was third overall with 81.1 per cent of flights arriving on time while service leader Delta had only 72.3 per cent of its flights arriving on time (Table 2.10). Carriers like Piedmont are advertising their service, meals and the introduction of first class in all their aircraft. Even Frank Lorenzo of Texas Air claims to be spending $1.25 billion to 'upgrade airport facilities and aircraft and to expand their fleet'. The overall tendency in the upturn/peak market is to improve service and raise yields because consumers are looking for just that (see Tables 2.11 and 2.12). In the next recession there will be an increase in fare wars that seem to last 52 weeks a year and the constant fight to cut costs. Those carriers that have been able to manage their costs best during the upturn will once again prevail in competitive wars. Therefore carriers will once again pay less attention to their products but be able to charge lower fares without losing too much money. As in all parts of the economic cycle, distribution will be key although the pressure to limit the costs of the distribution chain will be on again given that this is the biggest cost that has yet to be touched by the carriers. People Express began to pioneer ways around the usual chain of distribution but it did not last long enough to see these strategies through. Some analysts believe that when People Express decided to try and attract the high-yield passenger in the latter phases of their development, their previous alienation of the retail distribution chain was a contributing factor to their ultimate downfall. Direct marketing, shop-at-home purchasing, self-ticketing, frequent flier programmes and bulk volume discounts to best corporate clients will

Table 2.9 Consumer complaints filed against US carriers, by category (Oct. 1987)

Airline	Flight problems	Over sales	Reservations, Ticketing, boarding	Fares	Refunds	Baggage	Customer service	Smoking	Advertising	Credit	Tours	Other	Total
Alaska Airlines	5	0	0	1	1	2	0	0	0	0	0	0	9
America West Airlines	23	0	5	2	2	14	1	0	0	0	0	0	47
American Airlines	66	5	9	7	7	37	13	12	2	0	0	6	164
American Eagle	14	2	0	0	0	1	0	1	0	0	0	0	18
American Trans Air	3	0	2	1	1	2	0	0	0	0	0	0	9
Braniff Inc.	6	0	1	2	0	2	1	0	0	0	0	0	12
Challenge International Airline	4	0	1	0	24	2	0	0	0	0	0	0	31
Comair	7	0	0	0	1	2	0	0	0	0	0	0	10
Continental Airlines	246	23	52	13	83	98	55	9	9	3	1	21	613
Delta Airlines	53	3	14	7	10	12	11	2	0	0	0	4	116
Eastern Airlines	334	14	15	14	36	53	32	6	2	0	0	11	517
Eastern Express	5	0	3	0	1	2	0	0	0	0	0	1	12
Florida Express	4	0	0	0	1	1	1	0	0	0	0	0	7
Hawaiian Airlines	17	0	0	0	0	16	4	1	0	0	0	0	38
Horizon Airlines	2	0	0	0	1	3	1	0	0	0	0	0	7
Midway Airlines	15	0	0	1	0	2	1	0	0	0	1	0	19
Northwest Airlines	370	24	25	6	31	92	44	13	2	2	1	24	634
Pacific Southwest Airlines	7	6	1	0	0	2	2	3	0	0	0	1	22
Pan American World Airways	69	17	11	0	17	65	13	3	1	0	0	3	199
People Express Airlines	0	1	0	0	5	0	0	0	0	0	0	1	7
Piedmont Airlines	37	2	8	5	3	8	6	3	0	0	0	1	73
Presidential Airways	2	0	1	0	1	2	0	0	0	0	0	0	6
Sky West Aviation	3	0	0	0	0	2	0	0	0	0	0	0	5

The US marketplace 107

													Total
Southwest Airlines	5	0	2	3	1	7	1	1	1	0	0	1	22
Trans World Airlines	88	20	20	1	14	50	23	8	2	1	1	9	237
Transtar	1	1	0	0	5	0	0	0	0	0	0	0	7
United Airlines	122	8	26	9	15	67	22	6	0	3	1	11	290
United Express	4	0	3	0	0	1	0	0	0	0	0	0	8
US Air	37	3	6	1	4	16	9	4	0	0	1	3	84
Other US airlines	30	2	1	1	13	19	2	0	0	0	0	2	70
October 1987	1579	131	206	74	277	580	242	72	19	9	5	99	3293
Percent of total complaints	47.9	3.9	6.2	2.2	8.4	17.6	7.3	2.1	0.5	0.2	0.1	3.0	100.0
October 1986	257	78	63	52	132	177	45	38	12	10	1	38	903
Percent of total complaints	28.4	8.6	6.9	5.7	14.6	19.6	4.9	4.2	1.3	1.1	0.1	4.2	100.0

Airlines are listed if five or more complaints are received against them during the reporting period.

Source: US DoT

Table 2.10 Regularly scheduled carrier flights arriving late 70 per cent of time or more   (Sept. 1987)

Carrier	Number of regularly scheduled flights for which carrier reported data	Regularly scheduled flights late 70% of the time or more	
		number	percentage
Pan American World Airways	179	11	6.1
American West Airlines	526	27	5.1
Delta Airlines	2112	100	4.7
Pacific Southwest Airlines	526	24	4.6
Southwest Airlines	791	33	4.2
US Air	1092	41	3.8
Northwest Airlines	1313	44	3.4
Continental Airlines	1500	24	1.6
Eastern Airlines	1287	21	1.6
American Airlines	1871	24	1.3
Alaska Airlines	224	3	1.3
Trans World Airlines	812	8	1.0
Piedmont Airlines	1304	11	0.8
United Airlines	1788	10	0.6
Total	15325	381	2.5

Regularly scheduled flights are those for which the carrier reported at least 15 operations for the month.

Carrier	At 27 reportable airports		At all reported airports	
	Number of airports reported	Percent of arrivals on time	Number of airports reported	Percent of arrivals on time
American Airlines	27	84.8	111	84.5
Southwest Airlines	8	74.4	28	82.4
Continental Airlines	26	80.0	117	81.1
Eastern Airlines	26	79.7	82.0	80.4
Piedmont Airlines	23	81.1	88	80.3
Alaska Airlines	5	80.0	29	79.8
United Airlines	27	79.1	129	79.2
Trans World Airlines	27	78.8	85	78.4
Pan American World Airways	16	73.8	27	74.3
America West Airlines	9	72.9	41	73.4
Delta Airlines	27	73.0	118	72.3
Pacific Southwest Airlines	6	67.0	28	70.5
Northwest Airlines	26	69.0	108	69.0
US Air	23	66.9	75	67.4

Source: US DoT

all take on new momentum once again. Overall, marketing in the US industry will become like that practised in other industries. Marketing will also become cyclical in its objectives and predictable in content.

Table 2.11   The most important factors in choosing an airline

| | Length of flight | | | | | |
| | Under 2 hours | | 2–5 hours | | Over 5 hours | |
	%	Rank	%	Rank	%	Rank
Convenient schedule	67.8	1	59.9	1	44.2	1
Frequency of flight	33.8	2	13.3	11	6.5	11
On-time performance	30.7	3	22.0	4	16.1	10
Past experience	27.8	4	28.4	3	29.5	3
Low fares	18.0	5	19.1	6	22.0	6
Safety record	17.1	6	18.7	7	22.3	5
Attitude of personnel	16.8	7	21.4	5	23.6	4
Quality of in-flight service	15.7	8	29.5	2	38.5	2
Aircraft type	10.4	9	14.2	9	21.1	7
Availability of business class	7.8	10	14.1	10	16.2	9
Quality of ground service	6.8	11	5.8	12	4.8	13
National flag carrier	6.6	12	4.9	13	5.3	12
Quality of food and drinks	6.5	13	15.1	8	20.5	8
Frequent flier programme	3.2	14	3.8	14	4.3	14
Others	1.0	15	0.9	15	1.1	15

Source: Avmark Aviation Economist/IAPA

Table 2.12   Most influential factor in choice of a flight

| | Length of flight | | |
	Under 2 hours (%)	2–5 hours (%)	Over 5 hours (%)
Schedule	70.1	43.0	19.3
Airline	15.5	36.2	53.0
Fare	11.4	13.7	16.5
Aeroplane	2.5	6.6	10.2
Other	0.5	0.6	1.0

Source: Avmark Aviation Economist/IAPA

Conclusions

In looking at the US air transport market over the next 2–3 years, several things become apparent. The next recession will bring a milder repetition of the activity experienced during the previous recession in 1981–3. There will be more new entrant type 2A and 3A carriers in the next recession but fewer of them than in the last. The actual number will depend on how serious the next recession is. A minus 2 or minus 3 GNP growth will allow for a good number of carriers to enter the market. Few, if any, new type 2A and 3A carriers will survive the next upturn, however. Some of the existing type 1A carriers will not be around by 1990 and others will have been absorbed into other more competitive carriers. The next recession and subsequent upturn will see the establishment of fewer new hubs and an increase in hub wars among existing hubs and their dominant home carriers. The damage caused in the next US domestic downturn will be minimized for several carriers who have acquired significant international networks since the last recession. Carriers such as American, Continental, United and to some extent Delta will be able to draw on less affected international traffic which is partially governed by the economic cycle in the other nation. For this to apply to United they will have to speed up their learning curve on managing the Pacific network inherited from Pan Am.

Many analysts still maintain that United is losing ground to foreign carriers on many of these routes and with an increase of Pacific Rim competition the Pacific may end up hurting as opposed to helping United. The next economic downturn will only serve to excacerbate this problem.

Overall, many of the old strategies will apply but some new approaches, such as how to manage a hub war, or several hub wars at a time, doing a better job of competing with new entrants and striking the right balance between price and service competition, will all be part and parcel of airline managers' experience this time around. As in the past, the only constant will be change and it will occur at a faster pace as the recession worsens.

3 The international marketplace

'The present European system of air transport is illegal and I will campaign for unrestricted air travel throughout Europe'

Sir Freddy Laker, April 1979

'Where there is a sea there are pirates'

Greek Proverb

The feelings of Laker tend to reflect a general frustration on the part of air transport entrepreneurs who were tired of watching the big state carriers in Europe get bigger. The concept of US deregulation has been slow to spread and in fact many analysts will be quick to point out that deregulation could never happen in Europe. The word deregulation implies something quick, virtually overnight in the US experience, whereas in Europe the trend is towards liberalization. The term liberalization tends to imply a slower, more gradual pace in the move to loosen economic regulation.

Is deregulation for everyone?

The actual applicability of liberalization and the pace at which the reform should be undertaken is an issue that plagues many nations. We often hear of nations from Africa, South America or even some from the Middle East openly questioning the need for these economic liberalizations. How is one to judge whether a projected liberaliz-ation/deregulation will be successful? What criteria can be used to help measure that success? Is it more carriers, lower prices, more service, a higher quality of service, or all of the above simulta-neously? In generic terms, the points of reference that have evolved over the last 8–10 years seem clear. Even in the US, which has the largest domestic market in the free world, deregulation has led to consolidation and what some call an oligopoly. The actual level of competition, as measured in number of carriers in the market, has actually shown a net decrease in the larger carrier category. But the

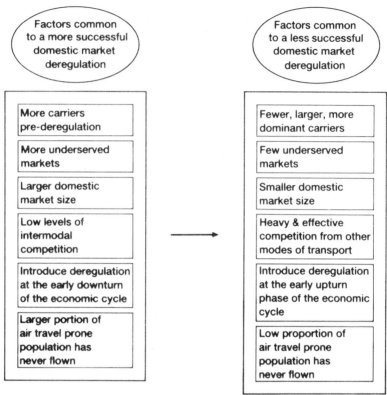

Figure 3.1 How successful will a deregulation of a domestic market be?

US was surely the ideal candidate on which to try out deregulation (see Fig. 3.1). It has a large domestic market, most of which is air prone (can afford to fly). It is a large country which tends to limit the effectiveness of competition from other modes of transport over anything but the shorter distances. There were many carriers already in the market while many more joined in after a combination of deregulation and the subsequent recession created many opportunities for new entrant carriers. The sooner, after deregulation of a national economy, that a country goes into the downturn of their economic cycle, the better for the new entrant. As the economy worsens the larger carriers start to hurt financially and their ability to compete with potential new entrants becomes impaired. In 1978 there was even a rather large dormant US air traveller market that had never flown before.

The lower fares of the 3–4 years following deregulation helped stimulate many of the Americans who had never flown. In 1978, roughly 50 per cent of Americans had flown whereas by 1984, 72 per cent of all US adults had flown. The annual air traffic went from 275 to 418 million passengers between 1978 and 1986 (*source: US ATA*). In other words, most of the conditions that were necessary to create a successful deregulation in the US were initially met. Measured in terms of its ability to generate more competitors, lower fares, more service and a greater choice of air transportation products for consumers, the US deregulation experience showed all of these features from 1978–84. As the impact of the economic upturn took hold, we started to witness the occurrence of carrier actions, which were normal in any unregulated industry sector, relating to the acquisition of market power and synergy. Cut-throat competition actually started to stimulate a move towards consolidation, fewer competitors and a tendency towards fewer, consumer-pleasing price wars. One must be clear on the expectations that a deregulation or liberalization actually generate. By unleashing the forces of the open market, it must be expected that the competitors within that market will try for financial survival and ultimately dominance. Therefore, the players will react in the way that the economic cycle, from which they are no longer shielded by regulation, forces them to. That means, among other things, more price wars in the recessionary phase and fewer in the good times. There is no one answer to the question of how deregulation will affect a certain domestic air transportation market but there are some parameters that can be used to project probable outcomes (see Fig. 3.1). Deregulation will affect any market in a dynamic and specific fashion that is directly tied to the local market conditions and characteristics. Therefore, it is not right to adopt a new air transport policy just because other nations have. The actual chances for success of a domestic deregulation are bound to be less than the perceived success of the US experience simply because the US had more of the factors present in its domestic market that could make for a successful deregulation than any other Western nation will. It remains to be seen whether the Chinese air transport system or even 'perestroika' in Russia will be bold enough to allow for free market forces to take over. Interestingly, the experience thus far has been that governments will invoke deregulation either because other nations did it or because the electorate think they want it because to them deregulation or liberalization usually means lower prices. The plain truth is that the US example has been picked up by consumer groups in all parts of the world. Despite this consumer pressure it does not necessarily follow that liberalization or deregulation is right for everyone. In fact there can be no question that many countries would be better off without it. Before looking at the European scenario, we turn to Canada's where proximity to the US has had an especially pointed impact on its domestic air transport policy.

Canada

Looking at the Canadian market one notes a relatively small population mostly strung out in a 150-mile wide band adjacent to the US border. The enormous size of the country (second largest in the world in land area after the USSR) means that competition from ground modes of passenger transportation is limited to short distances. Originally, there was a relatively limited number of carriers that were divided into four echelons. The two trunk or national carriers flew across the country and internationally while the five regional carriers were each assigned to a specific geographic zone within the country. In addition, there were some commuter carriers and several charter carriers. While the key impacts of deregulation (consolidation, lower prices) had been felt by 1986/7, the bill amending the National Transportation Act was only passed in January 1988. By then Canada had experienced a net decrease in carrier population (Fig. 3.2). All of the regional carriers, Pacific Western, Nordair, Quebecair, Eastern Provincial, Transair (absorbed into PWA), have been mostly assimilated into the new

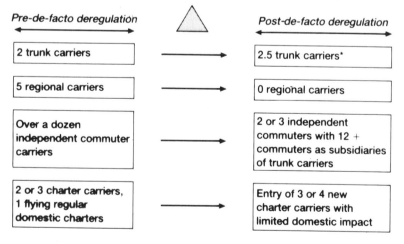

Pre-de-facto deregulation		Post-de-facto deregulation
2 trunk carriers	➞	2.5 trunk carriers*
5 regional carriers	➞	0 regional carriers
Over a dozen independent commuter carriers	➞	2 or 3 independent commuters with 12 + commuters as subsidiaries of trunk carriers
2 or 3 charter carriers, 1 flying regular domestic charters	➞	Entry of 3 or 4 new charter carriers with limited domestic impact

* Wardair in early development as trunk

Figure 3.2 **Canadian deregulation—industry structure shift**

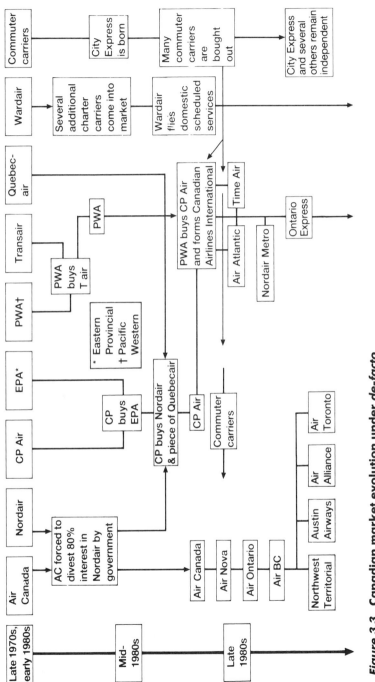

Figure 3.3 **Canadian market evolution under *de-facto* deregulation**

Canadian Airlines International Limited (Fig. 3.3). Air Canada has remained intact and a former charter carrier, Wardair, is trying to become the third national carrier. The fact that deregulation was introduced in the upturn of the economic cycle, contrary to the US experience, meant that the larger type 1 carriers in Canada were able to take advantage of their superior market synergy and to overcome the smaller regionals. By introducing deregulation in the upturn the government also made it more difficult for any (jet carrier) new entrants to come into the market. This difficulty of access was exacerbated by the relatively small number of high-density domestic sectors in Canada that were prone to market entry.

Since there are few sectors it becomes that much easier for the incumbent carrier to defend against incursion by a new entrant. In fact there have been no new entrants into the Canadian market, except for commuter carriers, since de-facto deregulation took effect 18–24 months ago (late 1985). Canada has had a *de-facto* deregulation ever since the route access mechanism, and its regulatory agency, were effectively bypassed by a series of carrier appeals directly to Federal Government Cabinet which saw fit to approve every application for new access. Similarly, most domestic fare filings have been practically rubber-stamped by the Canadian regulatory body, the Canadian Transport Commission (CTC), now The National Transportation Agency (NTA). The unofficial deregulation in Canada has really reduced competition, as measured by number of carriers, in the area of mainline jet operations. It has, however, spurned a growth in the number and size of commuter carriers. It is true that most of these new commuters are either owned by Air Canada or Canadian Airlines International Limited (CAIL) but the scope of this type of operation has increased dramatically. The market has gone from having three levels of carrier to having two levels.

The elimination of the regional airline has meant that commuter operations had to expand to pick up the slack in capacity to many smaller points that were uneconomically served by jets before deregulation. So what has really happened is that a majority of smaller sized communities have experienced more frequency but with smaller turbo-prop aircraft. Part and parcel of this trend has been an improvement in efficiency by the big carriers who can now pull jets out of smaller towns and redeploy them more economically on other denser city pair markets. Since the major area of change has been on the lower density routes there often is only room for one or two commuter carriers to compete. Therefore the limited increase in

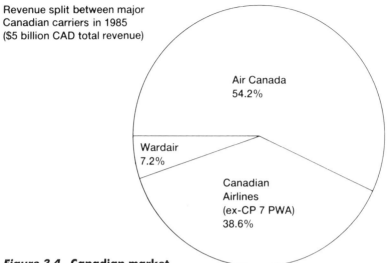

Revenue split between major
Canadian carriers in 1985
($5 billion CAD total revenue)

Air Canada
54.2%

Wardair
7.2%

Canadian
Airlines
(ex-CP 7 PWA)
38.6%

Figure 3.4 **Canadian market**

competition has come mostly in commuter markets not mainline routes.

Canada also happens to have one of the most travelled populations in the world. Consequently there was very little dormant demand waiting to be released by a move to deregulation. Therefore a synopsis of the Canadian experience shows a market evolution process that is all but complete, until the next economic downturn, even before the law had been changed in January 1988.

It also demonstrates limited success in achieving the prized aims of deregulation. The number of competitors has dropped, except among the commuter ranks. The fares had already been low and it would be difficult to credit Canadian deregulation with giving the consumer any significant incremental benefit thus far. One could say that while quality of service has dropped in many markets, from jets to props, the frequency of service with smaller gauge props has increased. In the next economic downturn the expectation is that one or even two new entrant carriers may decide to try and penetrate the limited number of city pairs where additional new entrant, competition might be sustainable. These will inevitably be type 2 low-cost, low-service carriers and will try to compete on price only since this is a segment where Canada has no dedicated competitors today. The ability of the potential new entrants to survive past the subsequent economic upturn is highly questionable. So the Canadian market is one that has not really enjoyed significant incremental benefit from deregulation yet, except perhaps at the commuter carrier level.

Other nations

Looking beyond the Canadian experience, we see similar scenarios in Australia and New Zealand. It seems that the markets most determined to have some form of deregulation are either members of the Commonwealth or have a relatively large but thinly populated geographic expanse to serve. The similarities between Canada and these two Australasian nations are striking. Both have few but dominant carriers, one or more of which are government-owned. All three countries have few high-volume routes into which new entrant competition could easily enter. In fact the early experience of liberalization in New Zealand showed that they had to go outside the country to find some entrepreneurs willing to set up a new entrant carrier. Australia is still grappling with the issue of reduced economic regulation but even if a full deregulation is enacted by 1990, as now projected, the practical impact will be limited at best. East–West Airlines had a small impact even before dergulation in Australia, although it has now been bought out by one of the other big two Australian domestic carriers (TNT Group/Ansett). Before its demise, East–West had only 5.4 per cent of the market while the two major domestics (Australian and Ansett) had a combined 86.8 per cent of the 1986 Australian domestic market share (see Fig. 3.5).

What deregulation means and doesn't mean
The 1981 Airlines Agreement, which enforced the TAP, requires three years' notice of termination. Consequently the government's new policy cannot come into effect until October 1990. This policy will comprise the following elements:

  (i) the removal of the controls over the importation of aircraft;
 (ii) the cessation of detailed determination of the amount of passenger capacity that may be provided by each trunk airline, and each regional airline which uses jet aircraft larger than 30 seats;
(iii) the abolition of the Independent Air Fares Commission and the withdrawal of government involvement in the determination of air fares;
 (iv) the removal of existing constraints on the entry of new domestic operations to trunk routes.

However, the government has been just as determined to spell out what deregulation will *not* mean. In particular, it has stated that:

  (i) economic deregulation does not mean that the government will in any way withdraw from, or lessen the effectiveness of, safety regulation. On the contrary, a series of new initiatives are proposed that will further strengthen Australia's already excellent aviation safety record;

1986 market shares

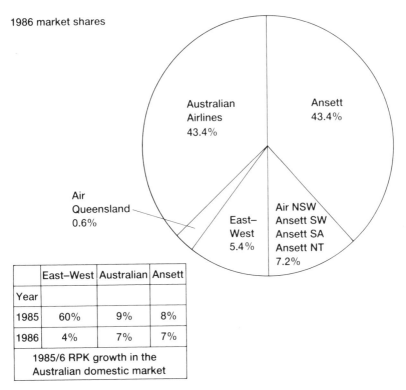

Figure 3.5 **Australian air transport market**

(ii) it does not mean that there will be any abdication of the government's responsibility for consumer protection or any lessening in its commitment to ensuring that effective competition prevails in the Australian aviation industry;

(iii) it does not mean that an open skies policy will prevail domestically insofar as foreign airlines are concerned, and in particular those operating international services to Australia; and

(iv) it does not mean that the government will abdicate its responsibility to ensure that its own domestic airline, Australian, is well equipped both managerially and in terms of capitalization to succeed in the more competitive environment that prevail from 1990.

Source: *Avmark Aviation Economist, January 1988*

While one can question the philosophical rationale for constraining competition, even if the Australian market were deregulated, within one trip around the domestic economic cycle there would probably still be only two larger domestic carriers, although the names of the players may change. Undoubtedly, the fares would drop, during the recessionary phases of the economy, with a type 2 carrier (low fare/low cost) such as East–West leading the way. The point is that the long-term impact would become cyclical as it has in the US. Every time there was an economic downturn, fare wars would start; and every time there was an economic upturn, the fare wars would lessen as the incumbent players would attempt to improve yields at the time when consumers could afford to pay more. Chances are that on the thinner routes within Australia (most of them) the actual drop in fares would be negligible because of the inability of many of these markets to sustain more than one large jet carrier, or two smaller commuter-type airlines. The net public fare savings benefit would accrue on the higher density routes and not on the thinner routes. Overall it seems that most nations with a large, thinly populated, geographic expanse to serve may enjoy a reduced net benefit from a move to deregulate.

Japan is yet another example of a domestic market where several are clamouring for a more liberalized approach (see diagram). While some actual loosening of regulations (market access) has occurred, there are still three dominant domestic carriers. Japan also has two regional carriers and four so-called exempt operators, but the fact remains that the big three domestic carriers transported 42.8 million of the 45.2 million domestic passengers in 1984 (Fig. 3.6). Interestingly enough JAL, the Japanese international flag carrier, which is somewhat restricted in its domestic route activities, is one carrier that would like more domestic access. Conversely, both of the other larger carriers, All-Nippon Airways and TOA Domestic, would like more access to international routes. Consequently, Japan seems to be spending more time concentrating on giving these domestic (and intra-Asian) carriers, All-Nippon Airlines & TDA, a larger international profile as opposed to deregulating the domestic environment at this point. Recent access to the US for All-Nippon and a projected push into Europe (London, Paris and Vienna or Helsinki are among points desired) for the same carrier indicate there has been some movement.

Outside Europe and the aforementioned nations there has been very little significant activity in the area of domestic market deregulation simply because markets are either too small, the local air system has not reached a level of development that can easily sustain the impact of a deregulation or because it is felt that the major government-owned carrier must be strong domestically in order to compete internationally. There have, however, been several non-

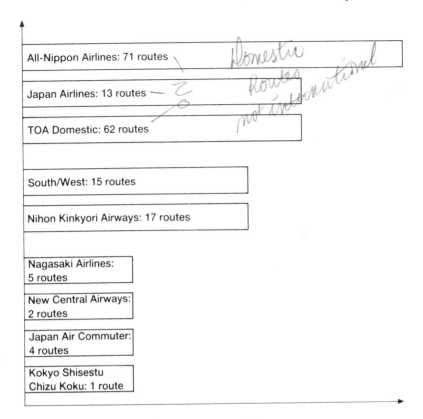

Domestic
Routes
international
not international

Figure 3.6 Japanese air transport market
Source: Avmark Aviation Economist

Western examples of a form of liberalization. In Russia the new open policy, glasnost, and the attendant economic reforms have spread to air transportation. Aeroflot is now offering certain performance guarantees to its clients with cash payment for performance that is not up to the prescribed standards. In China the former air transport system had one single carrier, CAAC, that was responsible for all air transport within China and international flights between China and other nations. The new system that replaces it has broken up the domestic air system among several provincial carriers that could be said to be indulging in a mild form of competition between them. CAAC is now relegated to performing international air transport duties with the new provincial carriers taking over internal services. While embryonic by Western standards, these liberalizations and service improvements do show a concerted move towards liberalization in many corners of the world.

We now turn to the current hotbed of activity, Europe. While the argument has been a protracted one, the tangible results have been relatively limited to date.

Europe—the traditional scenario

There have traditionally been three major carrier segments in Europe, the scheduled, the regional and the charter (see Fig. 3.7). Each of these groups of carrier fulfils a separate function in the marketplace although there is a high degree of cross-ownership between scheduled and charter, and scheduled and regional carriers. The scheduled carriers are typically government-owned and developed more as instruments of public convenience and necessity, as defined by the respective governments, than as entrepreneurial businesses. These scheduled European airlines have high-cost type 1 carrier structures offering full-service products to their clientele. The scheduled airlines operate within one of the most expensive airport and airway infrastructures in the world. This fact, combined with the carriers' own high-cost operating structures, have made for rather limited attempts at discounting. The yields must be higher in order to allow a relatively adequate return on many higher-cost shorter-stage length routes. The golden rules that applied in the US prior to deregulation are of course still in effect in Europe. Therefore it is still better to serve longer rather than shorter distance routes as the operating economics are better.

The second group has been the charter airlines. Nowhere else in the world has the charter carrier group evolved into such a dominant force in the air transportation system. These carriers have in fact become the type 2 (low-cost/low-service) carriers for Europe and in many international markets between Europe and other continents. The problem has been that these charter carriers tend not to fly on a regular basis nor on the routes that are dominated by business traffic as these markets have traditionally been served by the larger scheduled carriers. There are two groups of charter carrier: (1) the charter carriers owned by a parent scheduled carrier (Condor (owned by Lufthansa), Caledonian Airlines (owned by British Airways) Balair (owned by Swissair), etc.) and (2) the independent charter carriers some of which are linked to or owned by travel tour wholesaler groups. Finally the commuter carrier group has also been a substantive segment, more so in countries with larger domestic populations like the UK, France and West Germany. Intra-country carriage on the thinner routes has usually been provided by this group.

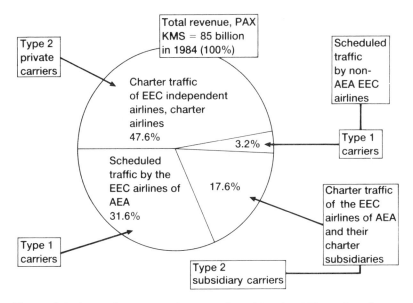

Figure 3.7 **Intra-European RPKs produced by the EEC carriers in 1984**

The dawn of change

Intra-country liberalizations

If one looks at Europe it is quickly obvious that effective intra-nation deregulation is not a plausible policy in many countries. Nations such as Austria, Holland, Switzerland, Luxembourg, Belgium, the Republic of Ireland, Portugal, Finland and others simply do not have either the geographic expanse or the population base, or both, to justify any move towards effective open competition on internal routes. The intermodal competition on passenger travel is quite stiff in many nations and the economics of setting up two or three carriers in these restricted domestic market zones are poor.

In looking at the 1986 IATA figures for domestic air carrier traffic (see Table 3.1) it is noted that Italy, Spain, Greece, Germany, Scandinavia and the UK seem to have larger domestic market sizes. The fact that Air Inter is not listed explains why France did not appear in the top twenty-one carriers; similarly, the size of the UK market is also not fully represented in the BA figures since many non-IATA carriers also participate in the UK domestic market.

Table 3.1 IATA* 1986 carrier rankings – domestic air traffic carried

Rank	Carrier	Passengers carried (000's)
1	United	47 788
2	American airlines	42 663
3	Eastern Airlines	38 988
4	Continental Airlines	18 691
5	TWA	17 216
6	Japan Airlines	9 253
7	Indian Airlines	9 176
8	Alitalia	8 184
9	Iberia	7 477
10	Air Canada	7 262
11	Saudia Arabian AL	7 170
12	Lufthansa	6 290
13	SAS	5 886
14	Mexicana	5 367
15	Australian Airlines	5 102
16	Ansett Airlines	5 063
17	Aeromexico	4 993
18	Olympic Airways	4 718
19	VARIG-Brazil	4 582
20	Pan Am	4 545
21	British Airways	4 269

*Many US and other non-IATA carriers not listed.

It is logical to assume that the best chance of setting up intra-country deregulation in Europe is within the aforementioned countries. Of these we know that the UK has already put a domestic liberalization in place. It has been criticized by the smaller carriers, however, because it offers very limited additional access for carriers other than BA to Heathrow. With the acquisition of BCAL by BA the dominance of UK domestic routes out of Gatwick may also accrue to BA although the terms which allowed BA to purchase BCAL left many of the Gatwick–UK routes up for grabs. With BA purchasing BCAL and having an interest in two other UK carriers, including Plymouth-based Brymon, it is quite dominant.

The independents such as Air UK, British Midland, Dan Air and other smaller scheduled concerns will definitely find things very difficult. The fact that Air UK has recently sold 15 per cent of its equity to Dutch-owned KLM was an indication that additional equity was required. In addition, Air UK has now announced that it will be getting into the inclusive tour market, which could either be a good insurance against failure of its scheduled services or more probably one of the few avenues for significant growth remaining for the regional carrier. The UK domestic air transport market has always had to compete with good road and passenger rail services, making the fight for lower yield traffic an even more difficult one. In addition, the hubbing effect of BA at Heathrow has had the tendency to steer UK domestic traffic that connects to/from other non-UK destinations over BA's network thus further limiting accessible traffic for UK local carriers. The extensive nature of charter operations on a point-to-point basis from many UK interior points also serves to restrict connecting traffic that local UK carriers could otherwise carry to an international hub. Overall, there have been several structural restrictions placed on any significant expansion by UK-based local carriers although increasing levels of service from UK provincial points to primary and secondary points on the continent may help these carriers.

Looking at the moves towards intra-country liberalizations in Europe, one would have to point to the UK as the most successful example to date. No other country has seen a significant expansion of regional jet service within their boundaries from new entrant carriers in the last 3–5 years. Most of the recent growth has come at the commuter carrier level. Despite this, countries such as France and Germany have some potential for domestic liberalizations. The internal market sizes are large enough although there are many factors impeding such activity. With Air Inter and a slew of regionals operating in France, many of them in cooperation with Air France, there may not be a move towards liberalization in the immediate future. Similarly in West Germany, the dominance of Lufthansa with its commuter links, including DLT and its cooperative arrangements with the German railway, seems an unlikely near term candidate for a major loosening of domestic economic regulation.

Recent trends in Italy indicate that all the new entrants are of the commuter carrier variety, with Alitalia and its domestic subsidiary ATI garnering the majority of the large Italian domestic market. Both Spain and Greece are known to have rather conservative views on liberalization and both are trying to bolster their national carriers. Declaring free exit/entry in their domestic markets would no doubt have a negative impact on these national carriers, although many of the intra-Spain sectors are money losers for Iberia today. Overall, there seems to be little activity planned at the intra-country level for the foreseeable future other than for the expansion of commuter carriers. Table 3.2 compares European carriers.

Table 3.2 European carrier comparisons

Carrier	No. of employees	Pax/employee	Passengers carried
Britannia	2 400	1 818	4 364 000
Dan Air	3 000	1 139	3 418 000
Air Europe	500	2 924	1 462 000
Orion	500	2 616	1 308 000
Transavia	560	1 444	809 000
LTU	950	979	930 000
Sterling	1 350	1 135	1 532 000
Braathens	599	3 172	1 900 000
Hapag Lloyd	760	2 329	1 770 000
Iberia	24 232	515	12 483 000
British Airways	36 189	429	15 521 000
Alitalia	18 144	431	7 824 000
SAS	18 258	561	10 251 000
Air France	35 232	341	12 026 000
Swissair	17 042	351	5 990 000
Lufthansa	32 535	430	14 070 000
Sabena	8 592	236	2 032 000
KLM	19 365	233	4 519 000

Inter-EEC liberalizations

When talking of liberalizing the European market, we are of course referring to inter-EEC liberalization. Most of the recent activity has been in the area of the EEC Council of Ministers and other bodies trying to get member states to loosen up the restrictions on increased market access within EEC nations. It is not my purpose to rehash the thousands of pages already written on the political and legal ramifications of the current fight to liberalize. Suffice it to say that there has been and is likely to be, until 1992 by current estimates, a major impasse on just how much or how little freedom from economic regulation should be allowed. The important things to remember are that: (1) The move towards less regulation, no matter how gradual, has started. (2) Many carriers in Europe have changed their strategies and are now planning as if there will be a liberalization. (3) Other global factors are having an impact on the movement in the direction of less regulation, including US deregulation (which of course could not directly apply in Europe), increased competition from Asian and North American carriers, and continuously mounting pressure from pro-liberalization forces within Europe. (4) Certain sectors of European aviation (commuters) have already been mostly liberalized making the next step that much easier. (This was a process that also occurred in the US with all-cargo and commuter carriers getting the green light for deregulation prior to the rest of the industry.) (5) There has been a global trend away from reliance on regulation to preserve carrier market shares to one that relies upon enhanced commercial understanding and activities to win the competitive battles.

Taking into account the current intra-EEC environment and the fact that it is bound to change at an ever faster pace, what are the strategic and commercial mechanisms that are and will be unfolding during the next 2–3 years?

Market Structure

While it is true that the U.S. environment and the various European air transport environments are different, it is also true to say that the industry structures vary as well. In the US there were three categories of air carrier as there are in Europe. The relative strengths of these types of carrier are quite different. The US environment was populated by high–cost, full-service type 1 carriers with very little to choose between them in terms of product quality. In Europe prior to the mid-1980s all of the major European scheduled air carriers were also of the high-cost, full-service type 1 variant (see Fig. 3.8). Since

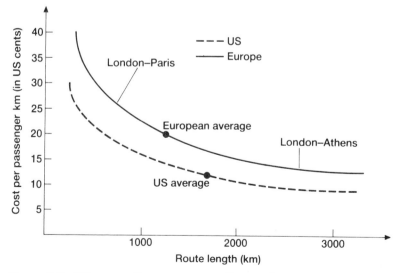

Figure 3.8   US versus European operating costs
Source: Airline Business, May 1987

the mid-1980s some smaller regional jet carriers have begun to gain market momentum although their growth has been restricted by regulatory impediments. The difference in Europe is that the various type 1 scheduled carriers do display a marked difference in brand quality. This differential has allowed certain carriers to garner higher shares of the high yield business traffic than others (Fig. 3.9).

The second category of carrier in the US prior to deregulation was the charter carriers, or supplementals as they were then known. In the US this group of carriers were a relatively small presence on US domestic segments when compared to the large importance of non-scheduled carriers in Europe today. The intra-European market share of the charter carriers has traditionally been around 60 per cent of the total passengers carried. In fact from 1971 to 1984 the actual

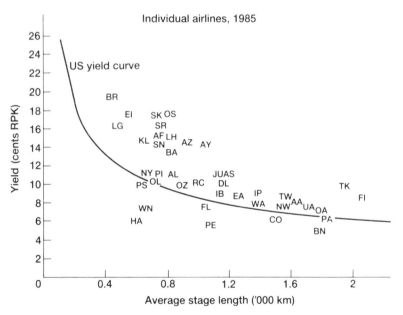

Figure 3.9 US and AEA yields–intra-US and intra-Europe

Key: **AA** American; **AF** Air France; **AL** US Air; **AS** Alaska; **AY** Finnair; **AZ** Alitalia; **BA** British Airways; **BN** Braniff; **BR** British Caledonian; **CO** Continental; **DL** Delta; **EA** Eastern; **EI** Aer Lingus: **FI** Icelandair; **FL** Frontier; **HA** Hawaian; **IB** Iberia; **IP** Republic; **JU** JAT; **KL** KLM; **LG** Luxair; **LH** Lufthansa; **NW** Northwest; **NY** New York Air; **OA** Olympic; **OL** Air Cal; **OS** Austrian; **OZ** Ozark; **PA** Pan Am; **PE** People; **PI** Piedmont; **PS** PSA; **RC** Republic; **SK** SAS; **SN** Sabena; **SR** Swissair; **TK** THY; **TP** TAP; **TW** TWA; **UA** United; **WA** Western; **WN** Southwest.

non-scheduled carriers' market share rose from 58 to 63 per cent of the total. This has been balanced by a loss of market share on several international sectors, including the North Atlantic. As a result of the loosening of tariff regulations and an increase in scheduled route rights exchanged in more recent European–North American bilaterals, the scheduled carriers have been able to grow their share of the overall market, especially since the early 1980s.

The third category of carrier that is common to both environments is the commuter carrier. As in the US the commuters in Europe have enjoyed a less stringently regulated environment than their bigger scheduled carrier brethern and share strong alliance links to the type 1 major carriers.

The three strategic waves

As a preface to the three strategic waves, it should be mentioned that the commercial environment in Europe will be fundamentally different from that in the pre-deregulation US for the simple reason that Europe has been able to watch what happened after US deregulation. The US had no similar example to study before they implemented deregulation. More importantly, U.S. carriers had no modern day example of proper strategic and commercial behaviour to follow in the event of an industry deregulation. It should be remembered that the airline business was one of the first examples of a US industry sector deregulation. Other industry sectors had their deregulations based on the experience of the airline sector: interstate busing, trucking, etc. all came after the airlines. The European carriers do, on the other hand, have many examples of company activity after an industry segment deregulation and how to react to rapid change. There have also been many examples of deregulations in other industry sectors within Europe that provide further data for the European carriers to study when plotting strategy.

Watching the early strategies and errors made by US carriers should have great value for European airlines as they try to navigate the same unforgiving competitive waters. Many of the marketing innovations such as major CRS systems, frequent flier programmes, yield management systems and the like have already been passed on to Europe and consequently the European carriers have better tools to face new entrant competitors than their US forerunners did. Similarly, any new entrant carriers have been able to watch the rise and subsequent fall of many of their counterparts in the US, so that the astute industry observer should be able to learn something from each one of those failures. Overall it should be true that liberalization will not be as much of a culture and management shock to the European carrier as it was to their US brothers. European carriers should make fewer mistakes and manage their assets better through all phases of the economic cycle. By the same token, the potential pool of competitors that will emanate not only from the new entrant category but from the strong existing type 2 low-cost, low-service charter (Eurocharter) carriers should provide a more formidable initial challenge to the major European carriers. It is also true that shock waves emanating from the US as a result of the mergers and consolidations phase of their industry evolution have been felt in Europe. Many European carriers are already reacting to this strategy, and the advanced perceptions surrounding mergers and acquisitions or other forms of cooperative commercial arrangement are developed to a more sophisticated level in Europe than they were in the US prior to deregulation in 1978. As a result it seems logical to assume that commercial pressure will lead political and legal reform in the installation of a more liberal competitive environment in Europe. It was the reverse in the US where many carriers were dragged, kicking and screaming, into deregulation in 1978.

The chain of events leading to more liberalization within Europe has been set into motion, producing the first three fundamental new strategic waves of commercial activity. While it is true that many of these activities have their basis in commercial strategies practised in the US, it is equally true that each has been adapted to the new environment in which they are being used. The first wave came as a result of the loosening of regulation on commuter carriers several years ago.

The major European carriers have been living with two types of restrictions in trying to develop smaller domestic or adjacent territory air services. The first are the regulatory restrictions that limit growth into new intra-European city pair markets. The second are the economic restrictions engendered by going into lower density markets that are uneconomic to serve using type 1 (high-cost/full-service) operating structures and larger jet aircraft. Both of these problems serve to restrict the traffic-drawing abilities of hub airports that are already embroiled in hub wars even though the official gun to sound the start of liberalization has yet to sound. Enter the commuter carrier that can perform the following services for the big carrier:

1. Generate good domestic grass-roots traffic feed from smaller

centres that cannot be economically served by the larger jet aircraft of the majors. In addition, commuters can provide increased off-peak frequency on medium or large-sized routes in order to maintain the market presence of the larger parent carrier by keeping service frequency high and pre-empting additional capacity from a competitor by blocking slot access at congested hub airports.

2.   Generate cross-border expansion, due to less restricted market access at certain sized airports within the community, and poach traffic for connection over the parent carrier hub as opposed to the hub of the major resident carrier.

3.   More efficient initial market penetration in low-volume markets, until they reach a juncture where they can be taken over by the parent major carrier which can then implement regular service with larger jet aircraft.

The application of the above strategies, which have been heavily implemented in the US and Canada, has not been lost on the European major carriers. A great deal of major carrier activity has been devoted to either acquiring equity in, or entering into major commercial alliances with, commuter carriers. The KLM 15 per cent equity stake in Air UK heralds a trend of cross-border commuter carrier alliances. Air UK was already the second biggest carrier at Amsterdam's Schiphol airport (aircraft movements). This equity exchange will probably cement and enhance the relationship.

KLM likes to say that it has the best global connections to most airports in the UK. It has poached many connecting UK passengers from provincial UK points for carriage all over the world. One suspects that this will not be the last example of cross-border investment in regional carriers by a major carrier. The consolidation and growth of commuter carriers in Europe has been significant over the last couple of years with most European major carriers now involved with a major web of commuter carriers on a variety of commercial bases from equity stakes to simple feed agreements. Lufthansa, Alitalia, Air France, British Airways, KLM and recently Swissair have all achieved agreements which enhance their commuter/regional level traffic feed.

The second strategic wave is the emergence of what are presently charter carriers into the scheduled market. While this strategic wave is still in its infancy, there can be no doubt that charter carriers could form a significant portion of the intra-European new entrant population in the coming years. The first sign of this activity comes from the UK where Air Europe has been very active. The recent route awards by the UK government have helped Air Europe set itself up in the scheduled business. With the purchase of BCAL by BA, the government has insisted that BCAL European and UK routes through Gatwick be put up for bids once again. Later BA made the comment that it would consolidate its British Airtours subsidiary with BCAL, now merged and called Caledonian Air and make Gatwick its charter airport. This would seem to leave a gaping hole in the scheduled market through Gatwick. If Air Europe decides to apply for and receives 5–10 more route authorities it could manage to mount a decent European hub from Gatwick. With its lower cost structure it could, of course, afford to charge lower fares and still make the same return as BA. In its initial venture into scheduled service on the London (Gatwick)–Paris route, Air Europe offered an £85 fare that includes a £25 in-flight cash rebate given to passengers (see Fig. 3.10). This low fare bargain could be one of the shots that will herald the beginning of unrestricted discount fares on intra-EEC routes. This is another phenomenon, like the commuter segment evolution, that will spread quickly, especially if Air Europe is moderately successful in its scheduled endeavours. The purchase, by KLM, of a significant stake in the Dutch charter/scheduled type 2 carrier Transavia may be their way of limiting Dutch-based type 2 competition.

The third strategic wave involves the growing uneasiness among the smaller carriers that are based on the fringes of Europe, so to speak. The growing paranoia revolving around mega carriers is spreading quickly. These smaller European carriers are beginning to feel that they may follow in the footsteps of Ozark, Piedmont, Air Cal, PSA, Republic and others in the US. Many of these smaller or medium-sized US carriers were very sound operations that simply fell prey to the old 'bigger is better' phenomenon, which in the upturn and peak of the cycle is a valid strategy for major carriers to follow. Over the longer period (5–10 years) there is little doubt that some form of commercial linkage will be present between the smaller and the larger carriers in Europe. The point is that there are many varied methods of linkage possible, ranging from actual equity transactions to feed, marketing, joint venture and other alliance mechanisms. This strategic wave may run its course before the next economic downturn because, as the US experience proves, conditions for an acquisition are more favourable for larger type 1 (high-cost/full-service) carriers in the upturn of the economic cycle.

The talks between SAS and Sabena and other discussions between smaller European carriers would tend to indicate that there may be

Figure 3.10 **Advertisement for Air Europe**

some activity before too long in this area. The difference between the US and Europe is that when there are talks about a larger carrier acquiring a smaller one in Europe, this has national implications for home country government of the smaller acquired carrier. For this reason it is not likely that we will see any mergers that represent a country losing its carrier. In fact, some kind of joint ownership of a merged operation seems more likely. This would not apply to an acquisition action between two carriers in the same country although, as the proposed BA/BCAL deal proved, the acquisition is not automatic even in these domestic circumstances. The final twist to this strategy would be a cross-border purchase by a private carrier of another private carrier, for example Britannia purchasing LTU or some such similar transaction. There would be limited political policy implications and a couple of mergers between several private airlines could create a formidable type 2 Euro-carrier. Overall, this strategy will evolve faster if the pace of liberalization is accelerated and the downturn in the economic cycle is forestalled for another 18 months. If the evolution of liberalization stays at its present tortoise-like pace and the next recession begins in the first half of 1989, this would have a dampening effect on this sort of activity. That is not to say it won't happen. Pan Am bought National while North Central bought Southern and Hughes Airwest (to form Republic) during a period of decline, even if these moves proved in hindsight to be rather major mistakes.

European industry structure—carrier types.

Leaving aside the commuter/regional carriers for the moment, I would like to take a closer look at the two dominant types of carrier in Europe today. Beginning with the type 1 (Eurotrunk) high-cost/full-service carriers (see Fig. 3.11), it can be seen that they have a rather similar structure to the US-based type 1s. Both have high operational costs, high fixed costs, high salaries, while inflexible job tasks characterize their labour resource. The fleets of these carriers are populated mostly by new, fairly young, aircraft. High debt and full service type products are other common traits between US and European type 1's. The factors that differentiate the two groups are the ownership structures, with US carriers being privately held while the European carriers usually have a majority of government ownership. European type 1s also come from different countries, not different states as in the US. While US carriers were more reflective of their American roots than their Dallas, Atlanta or Minneapolis home bases, in Europe the contrary is of course true. European carriers are not so much European as they are German, Austrian, Italian or French. Whether these carriers want it or not, consumers often associate the national traits of a country with their home carrier. Lufthansa must be mechanically excellent and punctual because they are German. Swissair must also share this endless

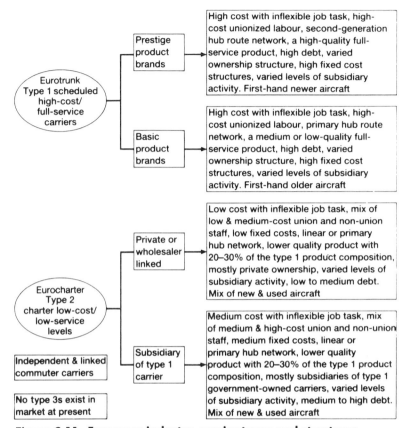

Figure 3.11 **European industry—carrier types and structures**

concern for punctuality and the Swiss fetish for cleanliness. As a consequence, the European carriers have gone much further in branding themselves and their air transportation product than the US carriers had prior to 1978. As a result there are two sub-categories of type 1 Eurotrunk carrier in Europe. The type 1 Eurotrunk prestige brand airlines are those that have accomplished not only a full-service product, which all type 1s have, but those who go beyond to have a high-quality, full-service product.

In order to deliver these higher quality full-service products these prestige type 1s have evolved specific characteristics of their own. A primary concern to many of these carriers is the state of their home base of operation, their home hub. Europe, as a consequence of geography and sovereign boundaries, has been forced to set up better, more sophisticated hubs faster than their American counterparts did: not simple primary hubs where a collection of aircraft come and go in a somewhat coordinated fashion, but superior air transit and passenger processing facilities. That is, an airport that is so ergonomically correct and passenger-friendly that passengers don't even feel as if they are being processed. A variety of features, including in-transit areas, large roomy holding areas, jetways, a large variety of services and of course a good schedule of flights and connections, all help to make the second-generation hub a different place to go through than the basic primary one. Building and maintaining these facilities is expensive but the carriers who have found their way into the prestige category have inevitably managed to afford them. Other factors that separate the prestige from the standard brands are their network, the state of their fleet, their punctuality and overall product image with the customer. Carriers in the standard category provide basic transportation with relatively few frills and an operation that may not be as predictable as that of their prestige type1 competition.

The second category of carrier is the type 2 (Eurocharter) charter carrier group. As previously mentioned, this group is much larger and more powerful in terms of market share than their US counterparts were at the beginning of deregulation in 1978. What is interesting is that the cost of production gap between most of the highly efficient European charter carriers and the European type 1 scheduled carriers is very similar to the gap that existed between the big type 1 US carriers and their new entrant scheduled type 2 (low-cost/low-service) competition. In other words, the market segment that was filled by new entrant carriers in the US may be at least partially filled by type 2 Eurocharter carriers crossing over to scheduled operations. This would mean a reduced role for new entrants in Europe and more formidable, better established competition from the outset for European majors. Within the type 2 Eurocharter category there are two distinct although subtle sub-categories of carrier (see Fig. 3.11). The first is the non-aligned type 2 that is characterized by low operating costs, a mix of union and non-union, low-cost labour with inflexible job tasks (not many pilots loading baggage here), mostly new aircraft and a primary hub or strictly linear route network which is of course variable in form from season to season. Other attributes include low fixed costs, private or wholesaler-ownership, a lower quality product (caters to bulk leisure traffic), and a varied level of subsidiary activity either directly or through the parent firm.

The second sub-category of type 2 Eurocharter is the aligned group, usually a subsidiary company of one of the bigger national flag carriers. This group distinguishes itself from the other by basically being encumbered with many of the costs of the parent airline. Consequently, the aligned type 2 has low to medium-cost labour that is more unionized than not. Inflexible job tasks, new or used aircraft (handed down by the parent firm), a primary or linear route network that fluctuates from season to season, government ownership (to same extent as its parent airline) are additional criteria for this group of type 2s. Certain infrastructural costs and overheads are often passed onto the charter subsidiary in some sort of pro rata basis that usually means that it has higher than usual fixed costs to amortize than the non-aligned type 2s.

These two groups of type 2 have varied abilities to operate as new entrants in the scheduled markets which could have an impact in the coming liberalization. The fact still remains that the major carrier type 1s could still use their charter subsidiaries to compete with other new entrants.

The next step is to try to project how these various types of carrier will react to a new competitive environment. Before even trying to project new directions, we can look back to the US experience to see that each carrier type had a better and worse time to grow. It can also be seen that each type of carrier had a more propitious time to consolidate and that when the timing provided by the economic cycle was ignored the consequences were rarely pleasant for the offending carrier. There is no reason for any of these basic rules of the air to change. One added difficulty in Europe will be that this zone is composed of not one national economy but many. Therefore, trying to observe the environment as a harbinger of strategic timing could prove even more difficult than it was in the US. The fact remains that most European economies will head in the same direction at the same time, consequently allowing the application of the correct cyclical strategies at the appropriate juncture.

Future carrier type strategic evolution

Starting with the type 1 Eurotrunks, we note that they will probably have some predictable responses to any liberalization. They will try to cut costs, raise productivity and match the lowest fares offered by the type 2 Eurocharter carriers in order to maintain price leadership in key markets. The latter action will, of course, prove difficult to sustain as the more efficient type 2 carriers will be able to make money at the lower fares while the bigger, less efficient type 1 carriers will be losing money on every seat they sell at bargain prices. This trend will be highlighted by any recession that happens to coincide with the early stages of any significant liberalization. Beyond this similarity, reactions to a significant liberalization in Europe by type 1 Eurotrunks will probably be very different. The ability to cut labour costs, or lay off many employees, will probably be restricted by the different socio-political realities in Europe.

Chapter 11 type bankruptcy provisions do not exist in Europe as such, so Frank Lorenzo would have had a much tougher time turning Continental around had it been based in an EEC member nation. By the same token, had Continental been based in Europe, Mr Lorenzo would probably have tried a tactic similar to that used by Mr Iaccoca in resuscitating Chrysler with government loans. Be that as it may, the fact remains that the European carriers will have a much more difficult time slimming down the human resource portion of their cost structure. The British Airways example would tend to suggest it can be done, however, if one doesn't mind golden parachutes (early retirement incentives) landing everywhere. The easier approach would be to try and achieve quick productivity gains and let attrition and early retirement packages handle the tough part of cutting the human resource pile. A serious recession may serve to curtail the options and speed up the process of eliminating unneeded human resources. As in the US, this will provide a pool of trained and lower priced labour on which new entrant type 2 Eurocharter carriers can draw. Many other areas of cost reduction should be attacked, including more innovative methods of fleet acquisition and management, elimination of unnecessary expenses, the pruning of route networks and even the sale of unneeded capacity (aircraft). Many of these strategies mirror those used by the US type 1s to raise their returns or minimize their losses, depending on whether they were on the up or downturn of the economic cycle. Another comforting thing to contemplate is that the likelihood of any major European flag carrier being allowed to go bankrupt, even if it had been privatized, is remote. A de-privatization could be a more probable solution to a carrier that becomes critically ill. So in a sense the potential outcomes of carrier management actions, good or bad, could not be as final as they had the potential to be in the US environment.

The final outcome for the smaller type 1 Eurotrunk carriers will be the necessity to align or cooperate on a commercial basis with one of the other bigger carriers. As previously mentioned, the tendency towards concerted activity in this area will be conditioned by whether or not Europe is having a recession or not. In a nutshell, then, European carriers will evolve by reducing costs and improving

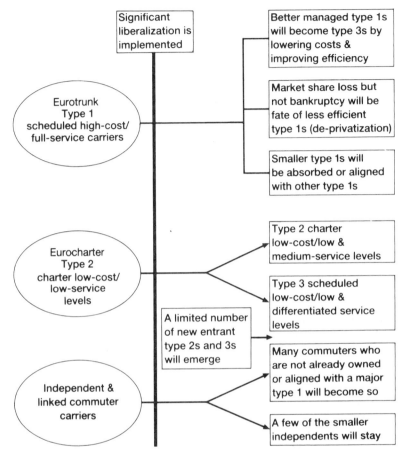

Figure 3.12 **Evolution of the European industry structure—I**

efficiency but they have a sort of safety net that protects them from the final catastrophe of bankruptcy. (See Fig. 3.12)

Lastly, the smaller type 1 Eurotrunk carriers have an additional worry as regards market size and synergy because Europe is not a single market as is the US. Turning to the type 2 Eurocharter carriers, there are several probable actions for this group. Some will decide that they are not interested in the scheduled market and will be content to remain experts at bulk leisure traffic carriage. This may prove prudent given the experience of the US supplemental carriers (charters), many of which tried to get into the scheduled market after US deregulation. Very few if any of those former supplemental carriers are around today to talk of their experiences. The new entrant carriers had lower costs than the charter carriers and were able to grow faster. The only trait, low cost of operation, that had segmented the US charter carriers into a separate niche had dissolved. In the face of open competition between the established US type 1 carriers and the new entrants, the charter carriers got caught in the crossfire. One can remember, however, that World Airways charged the lowest one-way unrestricted fare between New York and Los Angeles and people lined up outside their office to get a seat, for a little while anyway. This was before the People Express type carriers came on the scene. Some of Europe's charter carriers who decide to enter the scheduled market may very well get caught in the same competitive squeeze.

However, it is correct to say that some charter carriers have already gained experience in the scheduled market and that a more gradual pace of liberalization will keep barriers of entry high for new entrants. It may also be correct to postulate that any European new entrant will not be able to get the same cost advantage over the current group of type 2 charter carriers since they are more efficient than were their US supplemental carrier forerunners. Charter carriers such as Air Europe, which is already in the scheduled carrier business, may have an easier access to new routes until the liberalization brings on freer access to route exit and entry. Whatever the case, there will no doubt be some charter carriers that will concentrate on their charter market niche and avoid open confrontation with the big scheduled carriers. For those carriers who decide to enter the scheduled market, they will have basically two options. The first involves simply maintaining their type 2 status, low-cost/low-service mix, and adopting a scheduled type operation and network. As we saw in the US, this type of carrier, the same concept Laker originally had for his intra-European operation, will tend to do well when economic growth is low and consumers shift away from being primarily service-minded to an overwhelming price concern. This is the time corporate travel allowances are tight and executives start riding in the back cabin. In addition, there is the real possibility that low enough fares will start to shift people away from the well-developed ground traffic modes to air travel, especially over water (the Channel) or on longer distances. There is the potential to derive significant growth by intermodal shifting of passenger traffic. By the same token, the fares will have to be very attractive because the ground network of transportation is far more practicable/user friendly in Europe than it was in the US. This type of no-frills low-cost carrier will have the advantage of being able to cross-utilize the same aircraft and the same service components it does in charter services, thus increasing efficiency. This scheduled type 2 will be vulnerable to new entrant type 3 carriers that decide to have a medium and differentiated level of service while using the same low-cost base as the type 2. Finally, the former Eurocharter carriers turned type 2 scheduled carrier will also have to face the competition of any new entrant carrier that is born subsequent to the liberalization. Finally, the ability to cross-subsidize the new scheduled operation with revenues from the charter side of the airline may prove difficult since charter margins are usually thin. The second strategic alternative for the current type 2 charter carrier to follow would be to develop a scheduled subsidiary that offers lower fares and a middle of the road product with medium and differentiated service levels. Conversion to a type 3 scheduled carrier configuration would allow a better value product which will be more acceptable in the upturn and peak of the economic cycle. In the downturn and pit, however, segmentation of a separate service level (and the likely aircraft reconfiguration that will go with it) would be expensive when compared with the direct cross-utilization of charter to scheduled operations of the charter/type 2 scheduled carrier combination. (See Fig. 3.13.)

There is a group of jet carriers that has not been mentioned and these are the local carriers that have been present in the system for

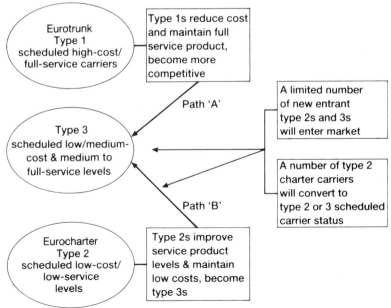

Figure 3.13 **Evolution of the European industry structure—II**

some time. These airlines include among their ranks carriers such as British Midland, Air Inter and others. It is a limited group that is even smaller if one considers those among them that are privately owned. Because of the small size of many of these carriers this group could be wiped out entirely by either a spate of acquisitions or competitive pressure from the improving type 1 Eurotrunk group or the emerging type 2 or type 3 groups of airlines. Despite lower costs than most of the bigger type 1 Eurotrunk carriers, these local carriers would have a hard time competing on price with a determined type 2 scheduled carrier.

Finally, a brief note about the commuter carriers. The two types among this group, similar to the type 2 charter carriers, will be aligned and non-aligned. The tendency thus far has been for commuters to have some kind of link to the larger carriers and this is expected to continue. The effectiveness of this group as an independent force based solely on commuter type markets seems limited. As in the US, most of the big carrier–commuter carrier relationships thus far have been based on commercial cooperation and feed agreements. Should the cross-border equity transactions between a foreign major carrier and a local commuter continue, there may be a backlash. The same phenomenon occurred in the US when larger carriers started improving the terms of a commercial agreement between a commuter and its original major carrier partner. The result was that the US commuters began to align with the highest bidder. The response from the bigger carriers was to get into equity arrangements that in effect guaranteed feed and the cooperation of the commuter carrier. In Canada there was a rapid buyout of commuter carriers when it was realized that in a country like Canada, where so many of the markets are low density, a national commuter feed network was necessary for both of the major trunk carriers. One has every reason to believe that a similar trend will perpetuate itself in Europe.

Strategies for success

Many of the so-called 'strategies for success' are being implemented by the respective carrier groups in a limited way today. The type 1 Eurotrunk group of carriers is pursuing, with varied levels of success, strategies to cut costs and improve productivity, although as a more significant liberalization approaches it will be necessary to increase the pace of these activities. The US experience proved that the large carriers do better in the upturn and peak of the economy. As this point approaches in the economic cycle in Europe, the larger type 1 Eurotrunk carriers should be attempting to mount as much growth as possible. Growth not only includes intra-European expansion but international growth outside Europe. Once again a variety of methods of growth are available each with their corresponding repercussions of cost and speed of growth. It is faster to grow when one pays only a fraction of the cost through a joint growth mechanism of some kind, especially when compared to internally generated growth that is accomplished by one carrier on its own. The amount of growth, and the budget available to do it, will allow various carriers to indulge in varied patterns of growth. What counts for the type 1 is that it grows when it can best afford to, at the upturn and peak of the economy. A final point for the type 1s to consider is what form of activity they plan for their charter subsidiaries. There are several activities that these charter subsidiaries could be used for, including the flying of some scheduled services in competition with type 2 scheduled carriers. The issue is what to do with these subsidiaries in the meantime, over and above their present functions. Making a pre-emptive strike at the Eurocharter carriers and making them fight for market position could also serve to dull their scheduled service ambitions, although many of the charter carriers have important cost advantages over the charter carriers owned by the larger major carriers which would tend to make this a short-term tactic at best.

These Eurotrunk type 1 strategies for a liberalized market would be complemented by a bundle of generically sound strategies that include the following (see Fig. 3.14). A key activity will be to re-orient managers who, despite their ability to observe the effects of deregulation via the US experience and that of others, will still need guidance as to how to manage in a much more dynamic environment. Further hub development is essential for all major type 1 Eurotrunk carriers. Even the prestige type 1 Eurotrunk carriers must continue improving their hubs in order to maintain their advantage over evolving carriers in the standard type 1 category. Computer reservations systems are an essential part of recent developments in Europe. The evolution of two key groups has resulted in significant streamlining of the CRS system. Another result is that the two camps (Amadeus and Galileo) may have trouble getting optimum product distribution in the other computer system's territory. The advent of home computer services and direct marketing tools may also affect the abilities of these computer reservations systems. The final generic strategy is an improved marketing ability at each of the type 1 carriers. The tendency in the downturn is to concentrate on price as the only variable. For the high-cost, full-service producers fighting a price war with more efficient, low-cost type 2 carriers is usually a losing propositon, or at best an expensive battle to fight during a recession. The US carrier group found that frequent flier programmes were a better lever for responding to price actions by lower cost carriers. The bigger carriers had a larger network synergy in their favour and one way to use it was to reward frequent users. This mechanism proved very successful in attracting and keeping sustained consumer loyalty. It was also a programme which the type 2 carriers, with their limited networks and flight schedules, could not match in terms of network synergy.

This was exacerbated in the US experience by new entrant carriers who seemingly only flew to obscure destinations. No one wanted to use their accumulated mileage points to get a free trip to a boring, cold or wet place. Amusingly, these programmes may be on the way out in the US due to pending tax regulations that would tax the

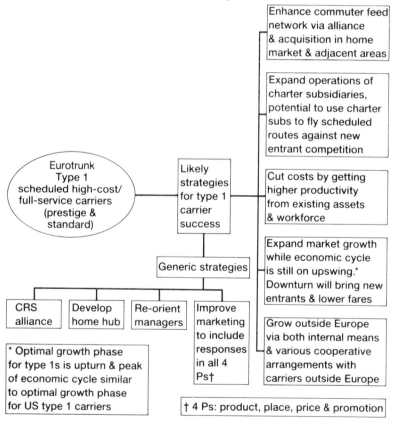

Figure 3.14 **European type 1 carrier strategies**

benefits flowing from frequent flier programmes. Recent innovations in the area of yield management also allow the bigger carriers to respond to low fares by introducing a capacity restricted fare at a similar (to new entrant) price level while allowing a higher proportion of high yield passengers to offset the expense of cheap fares. The ability to coordinate constructive action on all of the specific and generic strategies will be the core challenge to all managers at European type 1 airlines. The fact that some of these objectives are at odds with the others certainly will not make life easier. Figure 3.14 illustrates European type 1 strategies.

As was the case for the US low-cost/low-service type 2 new entrants, any European scheduled new entrant type 2 Eurocharter carriers will be navigating virtually virgin territory. While some examples of charter type 2 carriers getting into the scheduled market exist today (Air Europe), it is a limited population that has yet to make a significant impact. The key elements for an exciting competitive battle with the type 1s are in place. The gap in operating costs between the 1s and 2s (3s) is present. The insatiable desire for lower fares on the part of the consumer seems to be coming to a boil. (Table

Table 3.3 Promotional fares on intra-European travel, 1985 and 1986

Airline	Proportion of PAX on promotional fares	
	Jan–Sep 1986	Jan–Sep 1985
Olympic	92.1	90.2
Icelandair	87.3	87.1
TAP	80.6	80.3
Iberia	77.9	79.3
British Airways	69.6	68.8
BCAL	69.4	66.2
Alitalia	65.2	67.7
Aer Lingus	62.5	61.0
KLM	60.7	58.7
AEA (average)	60.6	60.4
Austrian	55.4	55.4
Swissair	53.3	51.7
Air France	52.2	52.7
Lufthansa	47.8	46.4
Sabena	47.8	47.8
SAS	45.2	44.4

Source: AFA (Association of European Airlines).
With the European major carriers averaging 60.6 per cent of traffic that travel on discount, and the US in 1986 averaging nearly 90 per cent, it seems clear that European carriers will experience a significant drop in yield after liberalization

3.3 shows a comparison of promotional fares for intra-European travel.) The upturn and peak of this economic cycle seems to be coming up shortly. The added excitement in the European market, relative to the US in 1977, is that there seems to be a ready pool of established type 2 Eurocharter carriers willing to enter the scheduled airline game. Many of these charter airlines have newer fuel-efficient aircraft and good wholesale and retail distribution networks. Many of the Eurocharter carrier names are similarly familiar to the sellers of air travel, making market penetration that much easier. However, there are some environmental factors that will tend to militate against the type 2s. The prime constraint will be that the market liberalization will not be all-encompassing nor will it occur virtually overnight as it did in the US. While a more gradual liberalization will constrain any plans for rapid growth on the part of new entrants, it will also give the larger type 1s more time to react to the open market which in turn will tend to improve their competitive resolve. Be that as it may, the new entrant type 2s will have to have a strategic plan on which to

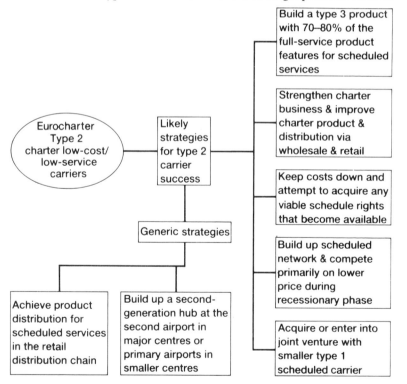

Figure 3.15   **European type 2 carrier strategies (private or wholesaler linked)**

base their attack on the European scheduled market. Such a plan will probably include among its various components the following elements.

One of the first decisions (see Figs 3.15 and 3.16) will be what kind of a scheduled carrier any new entrant wishes to be. As was the case in the US, the options are limited. A new entrant can either be a type 2 low-cost/low-service carrier or a type 3 low-cost/medium and differentiated airline. As previously discussed, a type 2 operation will have more in common with the current level of cost structure and service features on European charter airlines than a type 3 product which is traditionally a cross between the full service type 1s and the no-frills type 2s. One of the factors leading to a decision is the higher service expectation Europeans have in the areas of pre-flight, in-flight and post-flight product. This would tend to push new entrants to adopt a type 3 configuration. By the same token, the type 3 operation will be more expensive and less efficient (lower commonality) to run for the ex-charter based type 2 Eurocharter carriers. This decision point will be critical for all new entrants and will undoubtedly play a key role in the longevity of these carriers. A qualifying factor for this decision is that a new entrant carrier can always switch carrier type at a later stage, although a type 2 to type 3 cross-over seems easier than

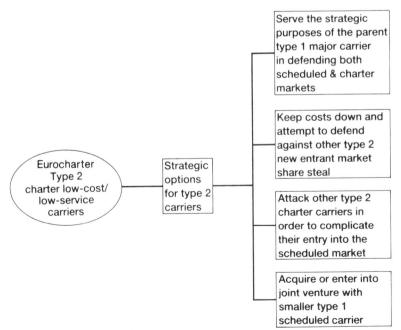

Figure 3.16 **European type 2 carrier strategies (type 1 subsidiary)**

the reverse. Depending on when the major liberalization occurs, it may be wiser to start as a type 2 (if liberalization occurs in the downturn). This would allow type 2s to compete better on price which is critical in the downside. The type 3 would probably be more suitable in the upturn.

The biggest challenge for any new entrant will be to build up its market fast enough to avoid being eliminated in the next upturn of the economic cycle by the bigger Eurotrunk type 1s. By the following upturn some of the ex-type 1s will have reduced their costs to the point where they will compete more effectively with new entrants. At this point, market size and synergy will become important (as in the US). The second option will be for the new entrant to adopt a market niche strategy and seek to strengthen their position within it. Sub-components of the market mass strategy are the selection and fortification of a home-base market hub. This will probably be especially critical since any carrier cannot just set up a market hub in any European country, at least initially. Chances are the sites for a new hub will be limited to points within one's own country making it difficult in some countries for new entrants to find a unique market hub to operate from. The options in other nations are good, however. Luton, Stansted, Orly, Dusseldorf, Munich, Hamburg, Manchester, Maastricht, Turin, Geneva, Lyon, Nice and countless others all offer relatively good hub startup points. The issue will be to set up enough frequency from enough points to get a good hub synergy going. A complicating factor will be that, with some notable exceptions, many of the present European hubs do not have overwhelming congestion problems which means the present type 1s still have room to expand their already strong hubs. The eventual congestion at these prime hubs will probably lead the type 1s to set up secondary mini-hubs which will reduce their overall efficiency and may push out a type 2 which had established itself there. The type of opportunities for new entrants in the area of hub construction will tend to be less favourable than was the case in the US, at least initially.

Another factor that the present type 2 Eurocharter carriers will not be able to lose sight of will be the health of their charter operations, unless a carrier decides to make a wholesale shift out of charter into scheduled service (an option that might appear imprudent in the early stages of the scheduled market entry by a former type 2 charter airline). It seems more likely that a certain degree of cross-subsidiza-tion will be present at least in the early stages. In order for that to be effective, the charter portions of these carriers must continue to grow and compete for the bulk leisure market despite the fact that the influx of additional cheap fare scheduled service will tend to shrink the overall market for charter type passenger operations. An added pressure will come from the charter carriers' subsidiaries of major type 1 Eurotrunk full service airlines who will be anxious to quash new entrants. The next strategic option that some present type 2 Eurocharter carriers (or strictly new entrant carriers) will consider is the acquisition of an existing carrier. This option offers quicker growth but, as we saw in the US, this strategy is best used in the early upturn of the cycle. The acquisition of a carrier would be difficult unless it was another new entrant, because acquiring an existing type 1 with its higher cost structure would not appear a wise move in a more price-competitive market. In addition, the only type 1s who are likely to be on the block are those who are in a less ideal financial situation.

The final strategic concern for the new entrant type 2s will be the need to enhance their existing methods of product distribution. The unaffiliated new entrants will not have had any presence in the market at all, making their distribution build-up task particularly onerous. As the European CRS network is becoming more of a restricted oligopoly, with Amadeus and Galileo distribution system penetration, it will become more difficult, despite the expected efforts of all, to make these two systems as unbiased as possible. An additional issue for new entrants will be that they will be forced to get into two systems to get Europe-wide coverage. This will, of course, be more expensive.

A different set of distribution problems face the type 2 charter carrier seeking to establish itself in the scheduled marketplace. Many of these carriers are already closely linked to or owned by large leisure travel wholesaler groups (Fig. 3.15). As such they have developed good distribution links with the retail level on the leisure side. Depending on what kind of product and resulting market segment the new entrants wish to tackle, they could have to develop a new distribution chain to sell their scheduled, higher yield oriented products. Developing a dual-purpose distribution system will be more expensive. On the other hand, if the charter-affiliated new entrant decides to stick to a no-frills type 2 product this distribution issue could be less onerous as it could avail itself of the existing charter side distribution to sell its product. The third group of type 2, affiliated subsidiaries of type 1 carriers, will have the easiest time because they will piggy-back on their parent carriers' distribution network.

The other sort of type 2 carrier, the type 1 charter subsidiary (Fig. 3.16), will enjoy most of the same strategic options and responsibilities, although their bundle of strategies will be less pure since it can expect influence from the parent. Influence by the parent will tend to project the charter subsidiary as a defensive mechanism used to protect their scheduled market share. Since the cost structure of these linked type 2s is likely to be higher than that of the private or wholesaler-owned charter carriers, the option of entering the scheduled market will be less attractive for the type 1 charter subsidiary.

The longer term future in Europe.

Much of the longer term future will depend on the combination of timings that accompany the liberalization. The phase of the economic cycle at which it occurs will be a key determinant. In addition, it must be admitted that a large portion of the future of European carriers will depend on how well they perform in international markets outside Europe. This contrasts with the situation in 1977 for most American domestic carriers. This issue will be dealt with more closely in the next chapter on globalization. Finally, it seems that on balance the chances for a successful European liberalization are about the same as those which existed in the US in 1977.

Main elements of the EEC December package

• Automatic approval of certain promotional fares falling within specified zones and satisfying certain conditions;
• An expedited arbitration procedure for fares;
• Multiple designation of airlines on routes above a threshold of 250,000 passengers per year (falling to 180,000 by the third year);
• A reduction in the capacity sharing restrictions where applicable to 55/54 in the first year and 60/40 in year three;
• Increased access on most hub to region and region to region routes;
• Limited additional fifth freedom rights, especially for Ireland and Portugal;
• Group exemptions from the application of the competition rules of the Treaty of Rome;
• A three-year timespan, after which further moves towards an internal market for aviation would be necessary.
Source: The Avmark Aviation Economist December 1987

The European scenario is different from that of the pre-deregulated US situation in that Europe has a stronger charter carrier population that lends itself more easily to type 2 (low cost/low service) scheduled market entry. Similarly the European scheduled type 1 Eurotrunk carriers were probably better segmented in consumers' minds before deregulation, than US carriers were. The

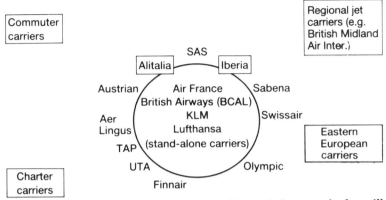

Figure 3.17 European airlines—who will stand alone and who will not?

difficulty for European-based competition minded carriers is that it does not appear that there will be a clear break between regulated and non-regulated market conditions. The more gradual approach will prevent overt and decisive marketing while protecting weaker carriers that are not ready to experience the open market. Another important question is how much market homogeneity will be present in the EEC over the longer term. Will Europe ever be one single domestic air transport market? Despite the potential for pessimism, many analysts maintain, and correctly so, that the trend away from the strictly regulated status quo of 5 years ago is now irreversible in Europe. The pace of freer commercial expression will be accelerated by the global trend away from regulatory protection and towards commercially based success (and failure).

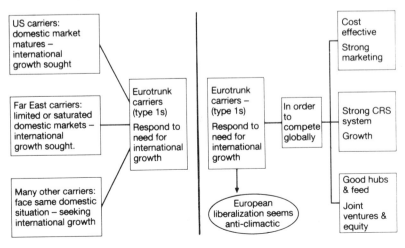

4 The globalization of the air transport industry

'If one were to remove (1) economic regulation and (2) the government ownership factor in flag airlines, international air transportation would become like any other line of business.' [39]

The global picture

With the US entering its second economic cycle under a deregulated regime and Europe threatening to embark on a serious attempt to increase commercial freedoms, is it not logical to assume that there will be a global fallout from these actions? In studying the constant change in air transport strategy, many would automatically tend to focus on various domestic aviation environments, notably the US. Normally, deregulation or liberalization are seen as natural precursors to change and in many instances this proves true. Despite this trend, the beginnings of a significant change in the outlook of the industry are manifesting themselves in the international environment in the absence of any significant liberalization there. It seems that many nations around the world are determining that their air transportation systems and carriers have reached the level of development that allows them to be released, even if only partially, from the embrace of government ownership. Up until the 1987 stock market crash, the trend towards carrier privatizations was nothing short of a flood. After all, air transportation is an expensive business and if governments can see their way clear to unloading some of the equity generating responsibility onto the private sector then why not? Table 4.1 shows the effects of the 1987 stock market crash on world airlines.

The trend towards strategic change among international carriers has been ignited for two major reasons. First, as more and more domestic markets become saturated with competition, thus making it more difficult to grow and generate a good return on investment,

Table 4.1   Declines in airline or aviation-related stocks. (stock prices)

	14 Oct	29 Oct	Change (%)
United States			
American	$51\frac{3}{8}$	$32\frac{1}{2}$	-36.7
Delta	50	$37\frac{1}{2}$	-25.0
Northwest	$57\frac{7}{8}$	31	-46.4
Pan Am	$4\frac{5}{8}$	3	-35.1
Piedmont Aviation	66	$61\frac{3}{4}$	-6.4
TWA	$30\frac{3}{4}$	$18\frac{3}{4}$	-39.0
Texas Air	$24\frac{1}{8}$	$13\frac{1}{4}$	-45.1
US Air	43	$30\frac{1}{8}$	-30.0
Allegis (United)	$102\frac{1}{4}$	74	-27.6
Boeing	$48\frac{1}{4}$	$37\frac{3}{4}$	-22.8
McDonnell-Douglas	$72\frac{3}{8}$	$59\frac{3}{4}$	-17.4
Dow Jones Industrial Index	2413	1938	-19.7
Dow Jones Transport Index	1012	725	-28.3
S & P Composite Index	3052	244.8	-19.8
United Kingdom			
British Airways	2.21	1.35	-38.9
BAA	1.50	1.04	-30.7
British Aerospace	539	368	-31.7
FT All Share Index	1199	856	-28.6
FT 100 Index	2323	1682	-27.6
Netherlands			
KLM	48.8	34.0	-30.3
ANP-CBC General Index	309.1	224.1	-28.5
West Germany			
Lufthansa	181	120	-33.7
Commerzbank Index	1496	1427	-26.7
Switzerland			
Swissair	1425	905	-36.5
Swiss Bank Index	722	515	-28.7
Hong Kong			
Cathay Pacific	8.65	5.30	-38.7
Hang Seng Index	3844	2204	-42.7
Japan			
JAL	19900	17600	-11.8
ANA	2360	2150	-8.9
Nikkei Index	26646	22034	-17.3
Australia			
News Corp	22.8	10.5	-53.5
TNT	6.54	3.0	-54.7
All Ordinaries Index	2306	1284	-45.3

Note: All share prices in local currencies.
Source: Avmark Aviation Economist

many carriers have and will continue to seek refuge in what was the relatively stable and regulated international market. This will in turn serve to destabilize the international environment because as a requirement for higher international market share becomes increasingly important to more and more carriers, then pressure will build for easier route access in international markets. A second consideration is founded in the costs implicit in more vigorous international competition. As carriers wish to grow they will have to acquire more aircraft, improve distribution networks to include new markets, expand route networks, improve their product, increase their support infrastructure, among other things. All of these things cost more money, and as competition increases the return on these newly acquired assets is likely to decrease.

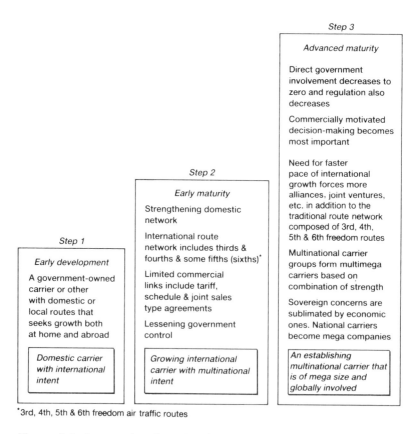

*3rd, 4th, 5th & 6th freedom air traffic routes

Figure 4.1 **International carrier development**

The increased costs of operation combined with government desires to withdraw from equity investments in airlines, let alone new cash infusions, forces carriers to find market based solutions for financing their growth. If the international market is taken as a single unit, then it can be noted that not all carriers have reached the same level of development. International carrier development tends to show that airlines are at either an early, early maturity or advanced maturity phase in their existence (Figure 4.1). Simplistically, airlines are born and first set about developing domestic networks (if one exists in the country in question) with a small interest in international air carriage. The next phase is an enhancement of the international network, once the domestic system has been adequately served and promises to yield little additional growth. Finally, the carrier in question has saturated the natural international traffic markets between itself and other countries and seeks additional growth by starting to partake in traffic flows between two foreign countries, either via its own territory (sixth freedom traffic) or between two points beyond its own territory (fifth freedom traffic) (see Fig. 4.2). As one may have guessed, the third phase of the evolution is a fragile one since the intermediate countries may get upset about a third party trying to implicate itself in markets that do not fall into its natural domain. Short of trading additional rights to and through its own territory, the carrier seeking to participate in traffic beyond that generated by its own market must find some other way of cooperating to obtain access to increased growth. The development of several methods of commercial cooperation have emerged as by-products of this need to expand and grow beyond the boundaries of natural markets. Having examined the steps involved in developing into a leading international carrier, let us pause to look at what types of carrier this international environment has generated. As a preface, it can be said that while most international carriers are not as experienced nor as advanced in their ability to manage according to market forces as US domestic carriers now are, some clear divisions between international groups have evolved over the years. There are basically three emerging types of international carrier (see Fig. 4.3) that can be described as follows.

International carrier types

Type A–the 'flag flyers'–remain traditional in their approach to airline operations. Furthering tourism, creating local employment, generating foreign currency and acting as a symbol of national status are all among the primary concerns of this group. Many of the flag flyers based in less developed countries have not yet met the basic public convenience and necessity covenants long since surpassed by

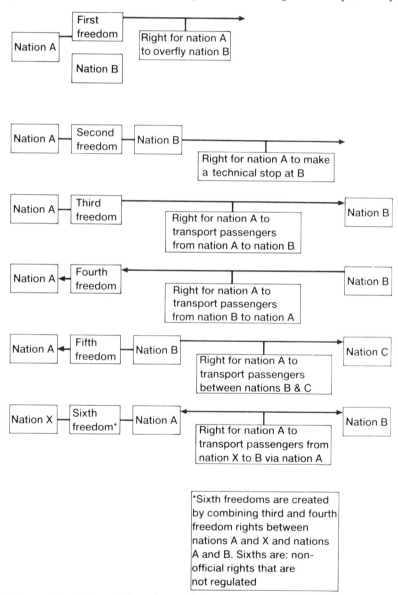

Figure 4.2 **Bilateral freedoms of the air**

carriers in other nations. Usually, type As operate fleets composed of cheaper but older aircraft on a combination of point-to-point third and fourth freedom traffic networks. These carriers often have the advantage of relatively low labour costs which are counterbalanced in

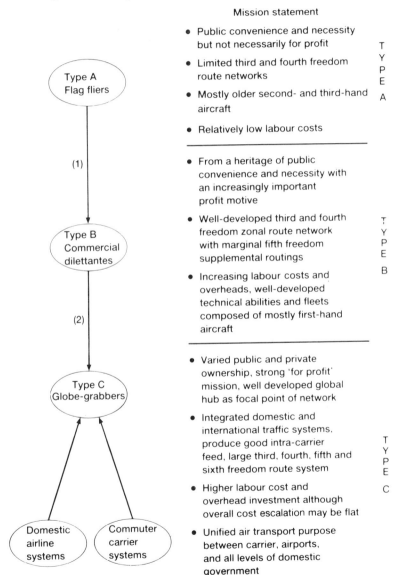

Mission statement

Type A
Flag fliers

(1)

- Public convenience and necessity but not necessarily for profit
- Limited third and fourth freedom route networks
- Mostly older second- and third-hand aircraft
- Relatively low labour costs

TYPE A

Type B
Commercial
dilettantes

(2)

- From a heritage of public convenience and necessity with an increasingly important profit motive
- Well-developed third and fourth freedom zonal route network with marginal fifth freedom supplemental routings
- Increasing labour costs and overheads, well-developed technical abilities and fleets composed of mostly first-hand aircraft

TYPE B

Type C
Globe-grabbers

Domestic airline systems

Commuter carrier systems

- Varied public and private ownership, strong 'for profit' mission, well developed global hub as focal point of network
- Integrated domestic and international traffic systems, produce good intra-carrier feed, large third, fourth, fifth and sixth freedom route system
- Higher labour cost and overhead investment although overall cost escalation may be flat
- Unified air transport purpose between carrier, airports, and all levels of domestic government

TYPE C

Figure 4.3 **Emerging types of international carrier**

many instances by a lack of local technical and managerial skills that usually necessitates the employment of more expensive expatriate labour. Most carriers begin life as a type A but may transit this phase quickly, especially those who benefit from favourable economic or geographic dispositions.

The relatively new Singapore Airlines (SIA) (1972) is a case in point. Being part of the former Malaysian/Singapore Airlines (MSA) prior to its present form gave it a good base from which to grow while its location on the heavily travelled Europe–Australasia corridor certainly aided its development. The other half of MSA has since become Malaysian Airlines which, while not growing at the same pace as SIA, is well on its way to departing the type A category. In general terms, the type A category provides the international air transport industry with its new entrants. The pace of development for these carriers is very often linked to the home economy. Therefore, although European-based carriers founded 40–50 years ago have long since graduated to higher levels, others based in less developed countries seem destined to remain in the type A category for a long time.

Following path 1 to the next category, we find the type B – 'commercial dilettante'– carriers. The majority of carriers from developed nations, and the overwhelming proportion of international carriers in general, find themselves in this category. Type B carriers have clearly moved beyond the simple 'public convenience and necessity' objective to one which is characterized by a great deal more emphasis on profit performance.

A major transition factor for these type B carriers, who aspire to become type Cs, is a change in corporate management from government-owned, populated by quasi-civil servants, to one of commercial entrepreneurs. This transitionary process can be a long one, taking two, three or even more corporate re-organizations over a period of years, before the shake-out is complete. The length of this shake-out period can often determine the relative competitiveness of carriers in the future. The rule here on the length of time between initiation and completion of the shake-out is 'the shorter the better'. While type Bs are struggling to reconfigure, other more advanced type Bs and type Cs are quickly leaving behind the type B in transition. Increased participation in traffic that is not necessarily destined to its home territory is the second factor that an evolving type B must become involved in. This involves increased development of its fifth freedom route network plus the development of a sixth freedom network. It should be remembered that many countries have the ability, in many cases presently dormant, to become regional if not international traffic hubs by building good in-transit facilities at key airports and developing domestic and regional feed networks; this is similar to the hub and spoke concept employed by most US carriers. There can be no doubt that the international expression of this hub and spoke strategy is more difficult to achieve because bilateral rights are required to build up the network, and successful negotiation of these rights is usually beyond the direct control of the airline. The third element required in order for the type B to progress to type C status is an adequately sized airline. Often as the type B carrier grows it becomes more sophisticated and its production costs rise, making it less cost competitive. Type Bs must cope with new growth to the point where they can offset the additional costs of competing in an increasingly sophisticated market by growing at an even faster rate, thus achieving better economies of scale. While air transport in general has never been noted for its return on investment, those carriers that have proper route structures in place can counterbalance losses of traffic or market share in one area by increasing their market share in another, just like multinational companies do in other industries.

Finally, other characteristics that a type B should possess before becoming a true type C include: a streamlined, young fleet composed of relatively few aircraft types; a large collection of route rights gained from bilateral negotiations; and a solid balance sheet.

The third carrier type is the type C– 'globe grabber'. This group is the elite of the international airline business. This does not mean that they are necessarily the largest but it does mean that they have used the arsenal of strategic tools at their disposal to permeate the international marketplace to a level that far exceeds the expectations generated by their natural markets. Part of the development of the type C involves a unity of purpose between the carrier, government policy (even if the carrier is not government-owned), the local civil aviation authority and the airport authority. This unity of purpose allows three or four interested parties to cooperate in making their carrier a type C airline. For example, what would KLM be without Schiphol, or SIA without Changi, or Austrian without its Vienna hub? All of these countries' governments espouse selective forms of liberal air bilaterals and so help to expand the rights of the resident type C carrier. And, by allowing their carriers to grow in this way, the governments benefit directly, or indirectly, from more employment, increased tax revenues as profitability improves, enhanced tourism prospects plus a higher level of resident technical expertise. As sophisticated market-oriented planning takes over at these carriers, the type Cs are rapidly becoming more like similar-sized companies in other industry sectors. Turning in a superior financial performance is no longer enough, however; these type Cs must aspire to some higher goal, attain more growth to offset rising costs and go beyond the type C carrier structure. As is commonly said, if you are not moving forward you are probably going backwards. The desire on the part of most larger carriers for increased access to international markets means that if the leaders maintain *status quo* they will be losing ground. So what is the next step beyond the type C carrier structure? This is unexplored territory in the air transport business, although some clues are offered by activities in other economic sectors. In all other lines of business the configuration which demonstrates ultimate success is the multinational corporation.

In fact a new pattern of multinational activity is emerging which indicates that the single multinational is no longer the ultimate. Paired or cooperating groups of multinationals are now the state of the art in market penetration and domination configurations. In industries from automobiles to computers to typewriters to heavy machinery, the last economic upturn has helped to stimulate far

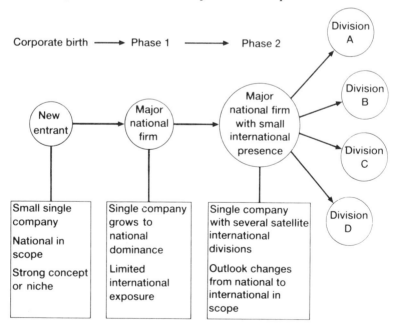

Figure 4.4 **Generic corporate evolution**

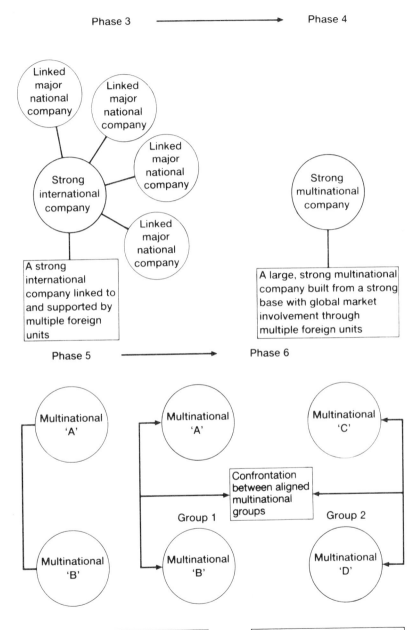

Phase 3 ⟶ Phase 4

Linked major national company

Linked major national company

Linked major national company

Strong international company

Linked major national company

Strong multinational company

A strong international company linked to and supported by multiple foreign units

A large, strong multinational company built from a strong base with global market involvement through multiple foreign units

Phase 5 ⟶ Phase 6

Multinational 'A'

Multinational 'A'

Multinational 'C'

Confrontation between aligned multinational groups

Group 1

Group 2

Multinational 'B'

Multinational 'B'

Multinational 'D'

Multinational growth is increased by using merger, alliance & joint venture agreements to expand quickly and optimize global market synergy

The final competitive scenario involves global competition between aligned groups of multinational companies fiercer competition among multinationals which has forced allied groups of cooperating or joint-ventured multinationals to fight each other for global superiority (see Fig. 4.4). As Mr C De Benedetti, CEO of Italy's Olivetti Corp., said recently, 'the traditional multinational approach is dépassé. Corporations with international ambitions must turn to a new strategy of agreements, alliances and mergers with other companies, if they hope to survive.'

As this global trend manifests itself in other industry sectors, air transport is justifiably far behind in this type of corporate development pattern. Air transport has not even seen the development of its first multinational mega carrier (multimega), yet! Why not? It is clear that there have been a series of blockage factors that have impeded the movement of the air transport industry. With a long heritage of regulation at all levels, there must be some doubt as to whether multinational carriers will be allowed to evolve. The problem for the more enlightened governments lies in assessing the net economic benefit or cost of surrendering their sovereignty by permitting their carriers to participate in these potentially monolithic organizations. The fact that most countries have already surrendered control of other industry sectors to multinational companies (and generally tend

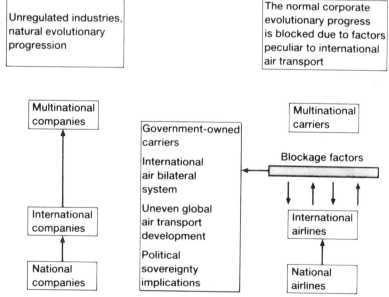

Figure 4.5 Comparative development of the air transport industry and other economic sectors

to regard multinationals favourably) suggests that some sort of economic trade-off is possible, especially now that so many governments are selling off pieces of, or all, their air carriers to private investors. There still remain other impediments that must be recognized, including the issues of uneven global air transport development that will tend to scare away many of the type A and newer type B carriers from a relationship where they will be dominated out of existence by a larger partner. The international air bilateral system, and the vast set of precedents to market access developed therein, will serve to slow down any multimega development until enough new precedents are set.

Sovereignty over air space, the military importance of civil airline fleets in times of crisis, the pride factor involved in having one's own national airline are all key tenets that tend to support the old regime. Still, there seems to be a renewed perspective when it comes to looking at how to assess the value of a nation's involvement in the air transport system. Spain, which has traditionally been involved in huge flows of air traffic but has had its national carriers transporting only small fractions of the total, is such an example. For a variety of reasons, many Spanish carriers, mostly the charter airlines, have been unable to compete on an equal footing with their European counterparts. The Spanish government was getting increasingly concerned about the low level of market participation by Spanish charter carriers so some changes were made. Today, because the foreign ownership rules were practically waived, many other countries are cooperating with private Spanish interests to develop new

> The multimega: A merger of unique strengths – little or no overlap or redundancy

> Intra-zone carriers: merge carriers of varied strengths (from contiguous geographic zones or nations), eliminate overlaps

> Transnational carriers: merging several weak carriers to form a single strong one

> Single carrier units

Figure 4.6 Strategic carrier merging techniques

entrant type 2 Spanish-based Eurocharter carriers. Spain benefits because even though ownership is accruing to foreign interests, its economy gains from having more jobs created, more investment, a greater tax base within the country, a chance to improve technical skills and develop additional pools of skilled labour, plus all the spin-off benefits created by the launching of a new entrant Spanish-based carrier.

In this case the way the Spanish government measures benefit derived from air transport activities has changed. It is no longer ownership in a certain traffic flow and subsequent profits, but the benefit derived from the creation of new carriers and, therefore, new investment in Spain. It is somewhat reminiscent of the process many nations go through to attract a new car assembly plant or some other industrial investment. This method of enhancing Spain's benefit from air transport has been repeated many times. A list of joint ventures to create new Spanish-based carriers includes: Air Europe (UK) and Air Europa; Lufthansa (West Germany) will cooperate in setting-up a new Palma-based charter carrier; LTU (West Germany) and Palma-based LTE; Aviation Finance Group (Luxembourg) takes 100 per cent of Spantax; the SAS tour subsidiary Vingressor takes a 23 per cent share in Spanish new entrant carrier Spanair; etc.

This different method for assessing air transport benefit to an economy could lead to many foreign-owned airlines being set up in other countries and is an important precedent in building up multinational airlines. There are several additional conducive precedents that have been visible for years in air transportation. International carrier merging strategies have taken various forms over the years and include the transnational carrier, the intra-zone carrier and finally the ultimate form, the multimega airline (Fig. 4.7). The first of these, the transnational airline, is alive and well as a primary form of carrier amalgamation. The genesis of the franco-African Air Afrique and SAS while not without problems have proven relatively satisfactory mechanisms for enhancing the competitive abilities of their component parties. These carriers are originally formed because two or more nations realize that they do not each have the resources to have their own national carrier and that a transnational carrier will greatly enhance what would otherwise be a series of very weak market players. Together these transnational carriers can compete with other type B and C carriers with much more success. These do tend to involve mergers of weaker components into a single stronger carrier. Other examples of this sort of arrangement are rumoured for parts of Anglo-Africa and other areas.

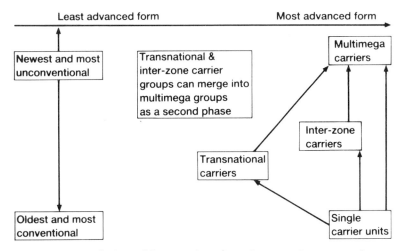

Figure 4.7 **Evolution of international carrier merging strategies**

The next type of carrier is the intra-zone carrier and this seems to be a category which is stimulating much interest at this time. The rumoured merger of SAS and Sabena and on again, off again talks between many European carriers tend to indicate that this form of carrier is a relevant strategic option in the near term. The merger of several carriers in the same zone has been talked about for many years with an Air EEC, an Air North America, an Air Asia etc. being the emergent global carriers that will compete internationally in the future. These groupings would be inferior in strength to the multimega since most of the constituent carriers would have strong networks in a common area while leaving large network gaps in other world zones. Fighting among the constituent members over who will drop what route and who will keep what route will reduce the efficiency of this type of configuration in the early phases of its existence. Similarly, we hear of Qantas taking a 20 per cent stake in Air Pacific, a carrier in which Air New Zealand already has a stake.

The third and final form of carrier amalgamation is the multimega airline. And while it may be difficult to go directly from single carrier status to being a member of a multimega conglomerate, there is no doubt that this can be accomplished by the larger more successful type Cs who reside in countries where governments have adopted an enlightened attitude towards change and innovation.

Multimega carriers are formed from carriers in different parts of the world who seek to merge complementary but mostly non-duplicating commercial strengths and profit. This bundle of unique commercial strengths is combined to form a strong multinational airline that is dominant in virtually all global zones and has the ability to insulate itself from domestic cyclical extremes by growing in other non-affected world zones, like multinationals in other industry segments. The evolution of these multinational airline groups seems natural in the competitive environment that permeates modern commercial endeavour. The fictional example of 'Royal Ameripore Airlines' is a good illustration of the kind of formidable type C carrier which can emerge from mergers (Fig. 4.8). Other such multimega arrangements are possible including another fictional group called United Anglo-Australasian Airlines (Fig. 4.9). Certain linkages already exist here including a common CRS system, between United and British Airways, the folding in of BCAL into BA network links between all carriers at strategic points and rumoured talks between Qantas and Air New Zealand on exchanging equity in each other's airline. Amusingly, when I originally wrote of the United/BA possibility I was not aware that two months later a major commercial

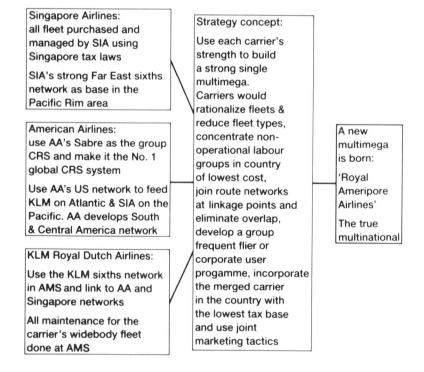

Figure 4.8 Example of a potential (fictional) multimega carrier

joint venture agreement between the two would be signed. As part of this deal, it is rumoured that Galileo (BA) could get up to 49 per cent of COVIA Corp. United's CRS system. In addition, joint use of common airport facilities, air traffic feed at common points and joint promotion are some of the benefits accruing to BA/UA in their deal. The attempt of a bulk seat purchase arrangement between American Airlines and Qantas in mid-1987 is another signal that carriers are seeking global linkage. One could posit a third fictional group called Scangenthai. Talks between SAS and carriers in the US and South America (it now seems that SAS will buy 40 per cent of Aerolineas Argentina) would support the evolution of intercontinental alliances. The recently signed joint venture, blocked seat arrangement, between Pan Am and Aeroflot for a joint operation with Pan Am aircraft between New York and Moscow also signals that these new multimega mechanisms can also be found in communist as well as capitalist environments. Figure 4.10 shows the global CRS competition.

A feed agreement (code sharing) between Continental and Transavia for US-Gatwick-Amsterdam traffic is yet another example.

What mechanisms lead to these multimega formations? In studying the development, four distinct stages of evolution come to light. The first level is the state of domestic government policy on international

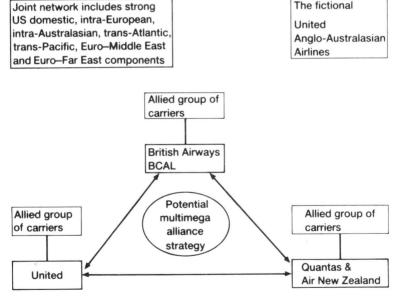

Figure 4.9 **Potential global multimega grouping**

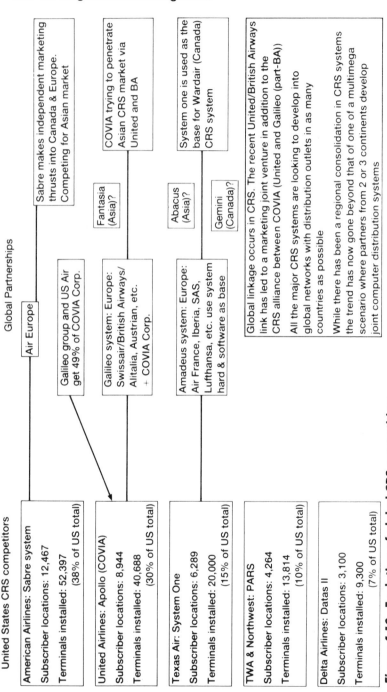

Figure 4.10 Evolution of global CRS competition

air carrier designation. Under this category, there are four possible configurations that emerge which include the following:

1. Traditionally consolidated countries are those that usually have one national flag carrier for all international carriage.

2. The newly consolidated countries which have seen a decline to fewer internationally certificated carriers flying from their countries. The ultimate consolidation is one which results in one airline per country. The UK has become a leading candidate in this category.

3. The traditionally fragmented nations are those that have determined that multiple designations are the best policy. Canada and France are examples of this type of policy.

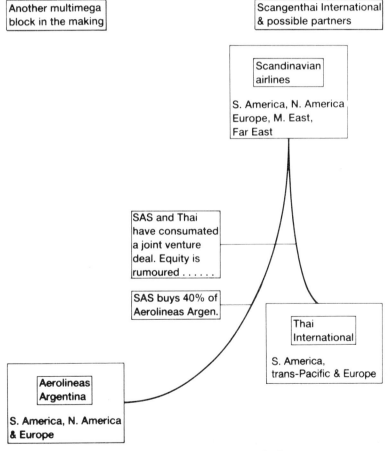

Figure 4.11 **Fictional carrier group Scangenthai**

4. The final group are those countries that have seen fit to newly fragment their international air carriage rights between two or more carriers. Japan, Hong Kong and the US are recent proponents of this policy.

The rules of thumb on best and worst options are quite simple here. In the future those carriers that have exclusive licence to operate from their country will be the strongest and best equipped to compete internationally. There are caveats to this scenario, however, in the case of the largest international travel generators such as the US who can more easily afford to have multiple international designations. A combination of smaller market size and multiple international carriers is a significant weakening factor for carriers from most nations. Most type Cs come from countries where there is only one international carrier and the first multimega airline will probably be the product of mergers composed of type Cs from one-country/one-carrier regimes.

The second phase is traditional alliances and the types of mechanisms implicit in this phase. These include feed agreements, captive commuter carriers, code-sharing, interlining, joint flight numbering and various forms of joint operation. These types of mechanisms are nothing new but the frequency with which they are being used greatly exceeds their past utilization. Many attempts at moving into new territory that go beyond traditional expressions of this type of transaction have been attempted or implemented over the last 18 months. The attempted KLM takeover of failing Air Atlanta or the attempted KLM/Florida Express code-sharing deal both had potential to break significant new ground and it is only a matter of time before similar arrangements are worked out and approved. Certainly as the pressure for international carriers to accelerate the pace of growth continues, these types of deals will be looked upon with more favour by governments who support their airlines' commercial aspirations (type C carriers).

The third category is the joint venture/equity arrangements type of transaction. There are several concrete examples of precedent-setting transactions that are rolling back the frontiers of commercial thought in this area. The BCAL/Sabena joint operation on the Brussels–Gatwick–Atlanta route proved a profitable improvement for both carriers. The silent-partner equity stake in America West by Ansett and the 15 per cent equity stake in Air UK obtained by KLM, plus all the equity stakes taken in Spanish new entrant carriers by foreign airlines, all point to an evolving trend here. Finally, having seen the activities in the first three phases evolve considerably, even in the last 12–18 months, we come to the fourth and final configuration and phase which is the development of the multimega carrier structure. The SAS/Sabena talks, BA/BCAL and others, as well as talks between SAS and Austrian and Finnair and the close relationship between such carriers as Swissair and Austrian, are all underlying trends that will surface at some point with the creation of a couple of multimegas. What is interesting is that multimega alliances in such things as CRS systems (Galileo, Amadeus) and maintenance pools are commonly accepted. Certainly the more strategically advanced carriers such as KLM, BA, Lufthansa and SAS are all trying to push ahead on these strategies. The use of code-sharing agreements in non-domestic circumstances was recently approved by the US Senate Appropriations Committee as a possible component of bilateral air agreements between the US and foreign countries. These activities are spreading as talk of a consolidated CRS system in Asia becomes rampant. In addition, another bundle of commonly acceptable multinational strategies are in place in several instances. The first of these is the concept of foreign labour sourcing which is common in many multinational companies. The American Airlines affiliated Caribbean Data Corporation is a prime example, as is the investment in Spanish-based charter carriers by foreign airlines because the cost of labour in Spain is among the lowest in the EEC. In the case of the Caribbean Data Corp., the data processing for American is done in Barbados at an hourly labour rate of $2.20/hour which is a good wage in local terms. The same job in the US would cost roughly $9.00/ hour. The net benefit to American is, of course, the lower labour cost. This allows the carrier to update management information systems at a much faster pace and at lower cost than would otherwise be possible. The specialization of different maintenance functions among ATLAS and other maintenance cooperatives is also another cost-saving measure. A further benefit of the Spanish charter carrier strategy for foreign carriers is that they are able to make a higher net return on low-fare bulk leisure traffic by using cheaper factors of production to carry this traffic (leased aircraft and lower cost labour). This is reminiscent of a strategy Volkswagen used in its car manufacturing business. The more expensive models such as their luxury Audis and similar higher yielding brands are produced in Germany where production costs are higher. The Polo, which is Volkswagen's economy model, is produced at the ex-SEAT plant in Spain, thus matching the lower yielding bottom-of-the-line car model with the lowest cost factors of production. In both cases higher yields result and effective product segmentation is maximized between higher and lower quality variants.

A differing level of preparation for the coming multimega thrust is, therefore, already apparent in various parts of the world.

Carrier types and development

The US scenario

When the US initiated its deregulation in 1978 it tried to accompany it with a push to liberalize the bilateral agreements that control access to international route rights between the US and foreign countries. Several of these so-called liberal bilateral agreements were signed and the US was the net loser on most of them. Countries like Singapore, the Netherlands and several other Pacific Rim nations all signed almost open-skies agreements with the US. The net impact was that the market share obtained by the foreign carriers went up in cases where a previous agreement existed or the new entrant foreign international carrier quickly got the main share of the market. Was the US wrong to open up international route rights to an open-skies policy? The answer is probably that the change in policy was a little early for the US carriers to take advantage of. After all, the US carriers had their hands full with local deregulation and the flood of change that it released into the US marketplace. Now that the US environment has stabilized, until the next market downturn, the US carriers have turned their minds to international expansion with a vengeance and are gaining market share in many areas.

Much of the market power that Pan Am used to be able to command came from its rather protected position as one of the two 'unofficial' US flag carriers. Along with TWA, it was able to focus its operations at JFK airport in New York and build up a major international hub there. During the 1960s and 1970s much of the international connection traffic flowed through New York. A combination of the disastrous purchase of National, in an attempt to develop a domestic feed network, a succession of union problems, an expensive to operate fleet which was compromised by having all three widebody fleet types at one time, and a series of management misjudgements and reorganizations all combined to severely undermine Pan Am's market position. Subsequent market developments in the US are now working against Pan Am which has been left out of the consolidation process. The new mega carriers are now seeing a significant reduction in domestic market opportunities as the dynamism in the US domestic market abates, until the next economic downturn. As some market sectors reach saturation additional infrastructural constraints have also appeared at the larger hub airports.

Strategic snapshot: American Airlines

(*Source*: *The Avmark Aviation Economist July 1987*)

In the fast lane of international expansion

Of all the carriers that have a chance of increasing their international presence, American Airlines appears to be the one in the position of greatest strength. The reasons are as follows.

● **Its corporate strategy advocates growth from within; American has learnt how to expand quickly and effectively, both of these attributes being essential in the international market**

● **Sabre provides a dominant product distribution network in the US, although international CRS expansion has been disappointing to date. Also profits from Sabre can bankroll expansion at American.**

American's transatlantic strategy

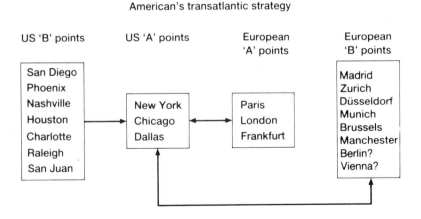

US 'B' points	US 'A' points	European 'A' points	European 'B' points
San Diego Phoenix Nashville Houston Charlotte Raleigh San Juan	New York Chicago Dallas	Paris London Frankfurt	Madrid Zurich Düsseldorf Munich Brussels Manchester Berlin? Vienna?

The idea is to build frequencies between US 'A' points which receive feed from US 'B' points and European 'A' points while developing links between European 'B' points and US 'A' points. As US 'B' points are developed they become new candidates for non-stop transatlantic service.

- American provides a relatively good quality of service plus a usually reliable on-time performance. The airline is now concentrating on a high-quality service image in order to fend off competition from low-cost Continental, and this will help it in the international market.
- The American Airlines Advantage frequent flyer programme will lock in members wishing to accumulate more mileage and the addition of more international destinations will enhance the rewards offered.
- The development of additional hubs means that American has excellent feed capability to support international services.
- American's two-tiered wage system, although under pressure, still means that new employees are cheaper to hire than existing employees. Given the higher yields on international as compared to domestic routes, this provides a double advantage to the airline.

A very powerful strategy is evolving at American. The carrier's international mini-hubs at Dallas, Chicago and, most recently, JFK have been maturing slowly, but American is already ranked as the world's number 13 carrier (3.4m international passengers in 1986). Transatlantic routes only accounted for 0.5m passsengers in 1986 but this was a 36 per cent increase over 1985.

It is worth noting the aggressive way American starts up service to new destinations—moving from zero to daily frequency, as on Chicago-Zurich, seem to be the standard market entry tactic. And originating its aircraft in San Diego on this Swiss route is typical of another American tactic—using twin engine widebodies minimizes the revenue penalty (from having too large an aircraft on the domestic sector) on the local leg and ensures feed for the international leg. This in turn, allows American to attract the high-yield passenger by starting up operations with a daily non-stop service.

In March, American bought 15 new 767-300s, all for deployment on international routes. By adding the 300 to its fleet, American can be flexible in deploying equipment to match market growth—for example, starting a service service with a 767-200, moving up to a -300 and then to a DC-10-sized aircraft.

American is also pursuing commerical ties in Europe and elsewhere to gain feed from beyond its existing European points. Part of this strategy has been AA's attempt to set up a Euro-mini hub at Berlin. American will show considerable growth on the Atlantic this year and stands to inherit a much larger transatlantic and transpacific role in the future.

All of these factors have caused an urgent search for new areas of expansion which, in practice, have meant international expansion. Northwest, United, American, Delta, Continental and even the US Air/Piedmont combine are all now operating in international markets. Ten years ago only Continental, Northwest, Pan Am and TWA had significant presences abroad. As a direct result of all this international expansion there has been an increase in direct trans-Atlantic and trans-Pacific services. JFK has had to live more on New

York–rest of the world traffic and less on the 'behind-the-gateway' traffic flowing through the city. With JFK's decline in relative importance, both Pan Am and TWA have had to diversify their operations by offering non-stop services from other US points. This development has reduced operational efficiencies of the two airlines and facilitated market entry by other carriers. Today, Chicago, St Louis, Denver, Los Angeles, San Francisco, Miami, Atlanta, Dallas, Washington and others have developed strong international traffic components supported by strong domestic feed systems.

The fact that US international markets are now being served through more gateways makes it more difficult for foreign carriers to wage direct market share battles. Growth for US carriers will come from stealing market share as much as from market growth increases in the overall market. This has led to complaints from foreign carriers about not having access to enough gateway points in the US. These complaints have so far fallen on deaf ears. Given the history of low market share penetration by US carriers on many international destinations, it is amusing that as soon as it looks like things may come closer to being equal that foreign carriers begin to protest. The trend towards minority market shares for US carriers will change. The newer US international carriers are in good financial shape, having excellent domestic feed complexes and rapidly developing the higher calibre service product necessary to compete effectively on an international basis. The ability to originate international flights at behind-the-gateway points is essential in supporting the frequency pattern required (if you are not daily you are dead) by the higher yield business traveller. The question is, which US carriers are going to survive in the international market?

Of the two traditional carriers, TWA looks to be in the strongest position with its acquisition of Ozark and the resulting domestic feed network and consolidation of dominant position in the St Louis hub plus its improved finances under Carl Icahn. Pan Am appears to be the likely loser and potential rescuers seem to be recoiling at the thought of assuming ownership of the highly encumbered airline. One look at its low value, old fleet, high debt and poor operating characteristics has led several potential airline suitors, including American, to look the other way. If Pan Am were to disappear there would be a void to fill and many route licences would automatically come up for bid among the remaining carriers. Given Pan Am's unhealthiness it would be cheaper and more efficient to let it die and then apply for as many route licences as can be operated. No matter what combination of US carriers end up getting additional route rights, the strength of the US international carrier group will have been enhanced. One thing seems sure: the strength and viability of the US international carrier population is healthy and that this group will be seeking market growth at a faster and faster pace. This can be seen in the recent applications by TWA, American and Continental to build hubs in Berlin, thus encroaching on the last US monopoly market left to Pan Am. Any one of the current larger US international carriers seems a likely candidate for multimega involvement.

The international scenario

Even if the European carrier group goes through a series of major mergers there will still be a significant number of carrier blocks left (see Fig. 4.12). Each block, after having reorganized itself, will be searching for new sources of growth. As European new entrant

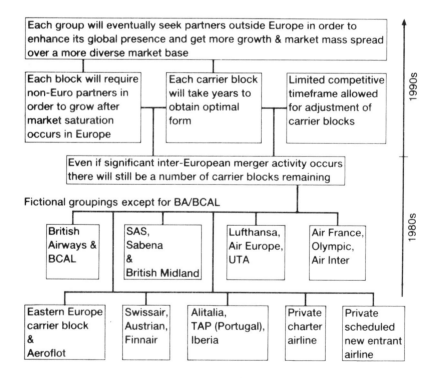

Figure 4.12 **European carrier development strategy**

carriers constrain growth and the eventual consolidation of the European carriers into blocks takes effect, the tendency, as is now the case in the US, will be to pursue new international growth opportunities. Most major European carriers have long been used to the fact that they must turn to the international market to secure additional growth, so this will be an easy to re-implement strategy. Increasingly tough competition between the newly-developed European carrier blocks will push to a search for multimega linkages.

In Asia we can note the possibility of equity exchange transactions between Qantas and Air New Zealand, the future links between CAAC and Cathay Pacific, the links between All-Nippon Airlines and US carriers, which are among the highlights in this region. Over time these carriers will also be searching for new growth through multimega alliances since most of these airlines have small or non-existent domestic markets which means heavy dependence on international growth.

In Canada the scene is one of a recent route swap between the two major international airlines, Air Canada and Canadian Airlines International Ltd. In this regard it could be cryptically noted that a similar route swap preceded the BA/BCAL merger action. Other than the aforementioned zones, it could be said that the tendency towards multimega type activities may be lesser in other zones although many have yet to recognize the importance of lesser developed countries in terms of providing low-cost labour and other cheaper national resources. An alliance with a Middle East carrier could provide a nice hedge against the rising costs of oil in an oil shortage, etc.

Overall, the geographic zones that are most likely to generate component carriers for inclusion in a multimega are North America, Europe and Asia (including Australasia). Each of these zones has a distinct advantage. The US carriers have a large domestic market on which to base their international expansion, plus they are relatively efficient producers, after being forced to trim costs as a result of deregulation. The European carriers are used to international competition as many have been forced to subsist almost exclusively on this type of traffic since their inception. In addition, they have good geographic positions and many of the world's better sixth freedom hubs are in Europe. The final group of carriers, from the Far East, have in most cases the considerable advantage of lowest costs of production. Therefore each of the carrier groups from these separate continents will bring to the multimega table some relatively exclusive but complementary assets.

Overall, the trend towards multimega development (Fig. 4.13), for the more successful carriers of the world, mostly from the previously mentioned world zones, seems to be gathering momentum. The issue now becomes: what are the best ways of positioning a carrier to take full advantage of these new trends? At the outset there will be a turbulent period of adjustment, similar to, although potentially far less dramatic than, the shake-out which occurred in the US domestic environment during the post-deregulation phase. During this period, carriers will align and adjust into the best multimega units that they can find. Unlike the US domestic carriers which are very vulnerable to the local cyclical extremes of the US economy, international multimegas which operate globally will be able to balance weakness in one area with growth in another. If the most advanced international carriers band into multimega carriers, what of the other 85–90 per cent of the world air carrier population that has not attained type C status? If proper multimega units are built among non-type C carriers, they will be more competitive as a group than they would alone. A multimega carrier composed of a group of type Bs would probably be stronger than a single type C carrier. The prospect of inter-type marriages are also present in the market. This would be the case where two type C carriers were looking for a geographic

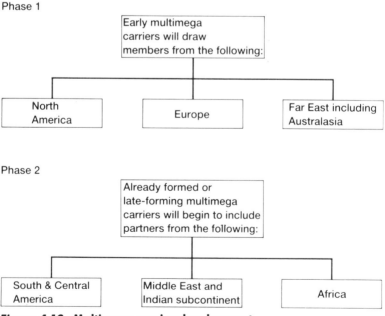

Figure 4.13 **Multimega carrier development**

coverage in an area where there were no type C carriers. Then an inter-type multimega could easily evolve. Finally, there will be a period of relative stability in the international environment after the multimegas have adjusted to their optimal form. This may be followed by a period of wars between groups of multimega carriers. This would be a similar evolution to the one referred to by Mr De Benedetti of Olivetti. Whatever the final outcome, one thing is sure and that is that there will be far fewer international carriers in 10 years' time than there are today. Even though the actual number of carriers will drop, the number of stakeholders in the system may not decrease since almost every nation will want to keep their hand in the multimega pie in some fashion.

The international future of air transportation.

I can recall that when the first article on the multimega concept came out in 1986 many were amused. It is, in fact, normal to be sceptical about a future scenario that predicates itself on drastic change to the present system. Maybe the multimega scenario would not be as strong an option if it wasn't a duplication of what has happened in almost every other line of business. Business is, of course, a strange outlet for human endeavour. After all, had someone said 15 years ago that The Coca Cola Company were going to take caffeine out of Coca Cola, they would have been laughed out of the room: many thought that caffeine was what gave Coke its distinctive bittersweet/cola taste. Similarly, had someone announced in 1965 that most cars in the US today were going to be of the small size variety, that would have met with equal amusement. Again, if someone had said in 1980 that IBM was going to be in big trouble by 1986 because of something called a clone, that would have prompted many a sceptical reaction. What of the Japanese, the Italians, the Germans and the Malaysians building cars under contract for the big three US car manufacturers? The sight of the international air transport business moving to a multimega scenario by the turn of the century may seem just as likely today as the proverbial cash cow jumping over the moon, or does it? By early 1987 several airline presidents were saying that mergers were going to be a key part of the international future of aviation. At an aviation conference in Montreal in May 1987, Dr U Nordio, CEO and Chairman of Alitalia, said: 'If one believes that US mega carriers are here to stay then smaller carriers have two choices…(1) try to stay in the big league or (2) accept downgrading and try to retain a safe niche in a local market. The first option requires the carrier to embark on the road of associations, mergers or acquisitions most likely reaching beyond the borders of its own country.' Lord King, Chairman of British Airways, used the mega carrier theory to try and justify the BA/BCAL merger when he told critics of the merger that, 'only our own national mega carrier can hope to compete on equal terms with the American giants of the skies.' In addition, many other airline presidents have been warming up to the concept. One of the staunchest proponents is of course Mr Carlzon of SAS who has guided his carrier to several sets of talks aimed at improving its transnational position through advanced forms of commercial linkage. Yet the scepticism persists in many corners. The reason for much of this scepticism is that it appears so foreign to the system known in the mid-1970s before all this deregulation and liberalization complicated things. The fact remains that most analysts agree that the industry has matured to the point, in most of the globe, that it can stand on its own. If the air transport business, like marine transport before it, decides to live on its commercial and operating knowledge then air transportation will end up like shipping has today, full of mega carriers. In addition, if one looks at the key trends that have characterized the airline industry over the last 55–65 years, the pattern that would allow a multimega development emerges (see Fig.

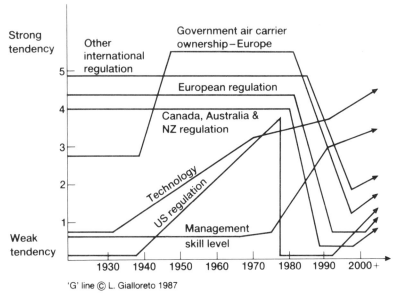

'G' line © L. Gialloreto 1987

Figure 4.14 **'G' line© trends for key air transport variables**

4.14). The various trends indicate a certain convergence of activity curves around the mid-1990s. Starting with some simple relationships, it is noted that the trends towards general global regulation were on the increase from 1938 onwards when the US re-regulated.

In 1978 when the constraining nature of economic regulation peaked in the US, it was still strong in the other parts of the world. Then things started to change, when Canada, the UK, routes between the UK and the Netherlands, several US international open-skies bilaterals and comprehensive re-evaluations of the viability of economic regulation in many other countries occurred. This indicated that the trend in regulation by 1984–5 was starting to swing the other way. The unique thing about the US deregulation was that it did not have any government-owned flag carriers to contend with. This was not the case in other countries, and the privatization of BA was seen as an inevitable consequence of the UK's internal deregulation in the mid-1980s. So the trends of government carrier privatization and less regulation seemed tied to each other, although some countries without significant domestic markets to deregulate privatized anyway since it allowed for greater access to equity financing for their carriers. Figure 4.15 illustrates the long-term aviation cycle.

Another relationship exists between the advent of significant technological innovation and the need to improve management skills. From the 1930s until the introduction of the Boeing 747 into commercial service, technology and the quantum leaps in efficiency

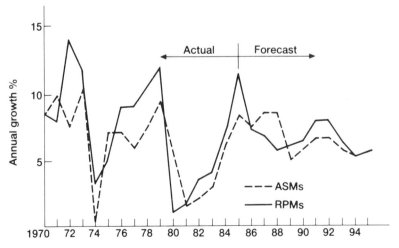

Figure 4.15 **Long-term aviation cycle**
  Source: **Merrill Lynch**

that it permitted helped the industry develop at a fast rate. It also removed pressure from the need to develop management skills relative to the push on this component in other industries. By the time the 747 had been in service for a while, and Concorde had settled into its limited commercial application to passenger transportation, the industry had built the largest and the fastest type it was going to need for the next 20–30 years. The growing concerns over noise and air pollution and the oil crises of the 1970s had forced aviation technologists to concentrate on building quieter, cleaner and more fuel efficient aircraft, not faster or bigger ones. The only thing out of the three criteria mentioned that helped the airline was the improved fuel efficiency, while the quieter and cleaner characteristics meant aircraft cost more money to build with little corresponding benefit to operators except the ability to operate into some noise restricted airports. Therefore the huge gains in productivity made possible by going from 200 to 450-seat aircraft were no longer available to airline management groups who were now forced to turn away from the technical side and to use their commercial and financial wits to achieve higher efficiency. The entry into the air transportation business of a number of non-airline-bred executives seems to indicate a willingness on the part of the industry to manage itself like other businesses do. After all, the recent innovations in air transportation have been more ingenious financing, or part-charters, or frequent flier programmes or better product segmentation, which have produced business class service. How can one consider in good faith an industry that consistently throws away 30–40 per cent of its highly perishable product, seats, every year. Any time a carrier consistently manages to use 80 per cent of their seat production, conventional wisdom would have it buy more aircraft. The costs of this waste are incredible and yet acceptable in airline circles. The advent of yield management systems is the first serious and systematic attempt to redress this mass wastage. These mangement areas are the zones of innovation in many companies. The cross-fertilization between industries has always been a source of what appear to be new strategies and products. After all, the frequent flier programmes were nothing but the airlines' version of the old S & H green stamps which one collected and then turned in for prizes at a US grocery store chain. It was a loyalty reward (bulk purchase discount) scheme just like frequent flier schemes have become today. Airline managements are being pushed to be smarter and faster than ever before. Aircraft technology no longer carries the majority of the weight of improving an airline. As airline management groups are forced to

look out beyond the traditional solutions, they are being indoctri-
nated into mangement practices in other industry sectors and trans-
planting what they learned back into air transportation. As the
collective outlook of airline management changes, part of the
measure for success will continue to be, who can grow fastest and
most profitably? Despite the bad return on investment reputation of
the airline business, things are improving. As a service industry,
airlines all over the world are putting the customer ahead of the
regulators in many instances and that is good since customers tend to
fly more often than the regulators. So overall there has been a better
balance struck between technology and the science of management
over the last 5–8 years.

So the trends are less regulation, more carrier privatizations, more
advanced management skills and an industry that seeks growth and
profits. Once growth outstrips the natural market size there will be a
tendency to align in order to continue growing and the multimega
carrier will be the ultimate expression of the need for the biggest
carriers to find more growth. What changes, if any, lie in the future
that may change this? Readers will note that by 1998–2000 the G
trend © curves (see Fig. 4.14) start to go back up, indicating that the
trends towards more regulation and even de-privatizations may
occur. This is a theory that comes from a look at the evolution of
man's need for transportation. Every time one gets into a new mode
of transportation that engenders colossal expense, governments seem
seem to be the only ones with pockets deep enough to foot the bill. It
happened with marine transport and even the railways in many
countries. As we have seen, the early costs of setting up an air
transport system were borne primarily by governments. Now we turn
to the next frontier, the next new mode, space travel, or at least
hypersonic air travel between distant points on earth. Who is going to
pay for this? Can individual airlines, as they are constituted today,
pay for these aircraft which could cost anywhere from $500 million to
$700 million each (four to seven times the cost of a single 747)? More
importantly, can the manufacturers who plan to build them afford it?
With projected development costs for a hypersonic design that could
run from $10–20 billion, this has to be a major concern (Boeing spent
$3 billion to develop both the Boeing 757 and 767 aircraft). What will
it cost to fly on these aircraft and will there be the necessity of some
kind of subsidy to build and operate this type of aircraft as there was
with the Concorde? Several carriers including Lufthansa suggest that
the passengers on this type of aircraft will be at least full fare
economy type passengers as airlines could not afford to put discount

passengers on such an expensive aircraft. The question is: with supersonic Concorde fares running at roughly 160 percent of first-class fares will that make hypersonic air fares 320 percent of full first-class fares (double the speed, double the fare !)? Passengers could end up paying by the Mach number as opposed to a formula that bases itself on distance travelled. The entire industry tariff machinery would be turned upside down. According to Lufthansa even if the hypersonic types of aircraft were able to capture 75 percent of all international first class travel and 50 percent of business-class air travel there would be a need for a maximum of 55–69 hypersonic aircraft or 92–115 second-generation supersonic aircraft in the world which is far fewer than the 400 sales that manufacturers figure they would need to break even. The operation of such ultra-high technology aircraft may prove to be beyond the means of a single airline. In fact a scenario has already been developed whereby several carriers

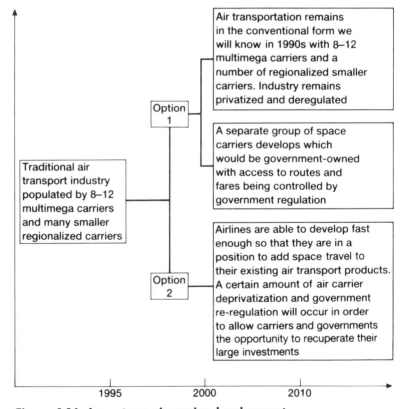

Figure 4.16 **Long-term air carrier development**

(or one multimega carrier) can pool operations on a single aircraft [36]. 'For example, British Airways, if that is what it is still called in 1998 or 2000, might fly a hypersonic aircraft from London to Hong Kong, where the plane could be transferred to Cathay Pacific for a roundtrip from Hong Kong to San Francisco. British Airways flight crews could reclaim the plane in Hong Kong for the hypersonic trip back to London [37].' Figure 4.16 illustrates long-term carrier development.

Clearly this new technology is exciting but it also has a very high risk attached to it that could easily bankrupt an airline. The issue is, which international carriers will be able to afford it in the first place? In fact, the multimega carriers that are projected to populate the air transportation business may have amassed large enough market shares spread over the globe that they will not only be able to buy, or lease, these hypersonics but will also have enough demand on ultra-long-stage routes to make a good return on such expensive aircraft. Interestingly, the advent of a viable hypersonic aircraft will make point-to-point flying on long-haul routes viable. Consequently those nations that have good domestic market bases to draw from will want to preserve them for their home carriers, or the multimega carriers that will be based in their country at that time. There could very well be a renewed protectionist tendency in order to help locally based carriers. Governments, as in the past, will have to become involved because of the huge air transport system infrastructural changes that will be necessitated by aircraft that can't use the airports or the types of fuel we have today. The mammoth new equity investment required to develop both the aircraft and the system to handle it could lead to a renewed government involvement in air transportation. Returning to the G line © trend curves, we note that both government involvement, as well as the level of regulation, will start to increase. Theoretically, as governments invest more and more in developing these new hypersonics and the required infrastructure they may ask for an equity stake in the manufacturers who build them and the airlines who require government-sponsored financing to buy them. The continued growth of the so-called mega-leasing companies has prompted such groups as Guiness Peat to say they might buy hypersonics to lease out to willing operators or the several willing operators needed in order to be able to afford that monthly lease payment.

Many of the strategies discussed in this chapter are in their infancy. and only time can vindicate their prognosticator. Be that as it may, Europe is getting ready to break new ground in the areas of free market management as have Canada, the UK domestic market and others.

It is clear that the changes proposed by the concept of multimega carriers and globalization may seem outlandish to the conservative managers in many corners of the industry. Some simple practical facts will serve to stimulate the pace of change, however. Air transportation has and will continue to become more and more of a global industry. Carriers that operated in exclusively domestic markets are growing into the international sphere and carriers who were already international operators are growing into new markets. The larger international carriers are fighting harder to maintain a share in existing markets and compensating for any resulting loss in revenues by entering new markets in order to maintain growth. As globalized market interaction occurs there will be commercial market share and revenue wars between carriers who have various operating structures. The US carriers, and privatized carriers from other nations will have a better chance of excelling because they will have the commercial freedom to operate in a 'for-profit' mode while government-owned carriers will continue to be encumbered by the non-commercial attitude of stakeholder governments and may have difficulty raising the necessary equity to compete effectively. One of two things will result; either the inefficient government-owned carrier will lose market share and revenues, or it will find a way of getting itself privatized. An alternative open to the government which owns a carrier that is underperforming would be to exercise protectionist measures to safeguard its carriers from the ravages of over-zealous competition. The problem with the adoption of a protectionist attitude would be that further growth required to get the carrier in question back into shape may be cut off because other governments may retaliate against that country by exercising protectionist actions against its carriers.

In short, it would seem that the trend towards the commercial era of international aviation is formally entrenched. As such, the industry players will slowly be converted from their previous prime objective of 'public convenience and necessity' to one which seeks profit. As more and more of the industry players are converted it will become increasingly difficult for the others to ignore the trend. The resultant 'domino effect' will see the big getting bigger and the multinational corporations of the airline business, the multimega carrier, develop. This sort of prediction would conform to the air transport industry life cycle that has developed up to 1988. The industry is in its early/mid maturity stage. Comparisons with other industries would suggest the time is ripe for mega-sized corporations, the like of which the industry has not yet seen. As time goes on, air transport becomes more and more like any other capital-intensive, service-oriented line of business. The biggest wave of change will be the commercial renaissance of the global air transport business. After all, this industry started on the backs of trail-blazing entrepreneurs who counted the sums paid for every gallon of fuel as a major cost item. In developing a uniform standard of safe air operations and in evolving the global air transportation system as we know it today, there was the requirement for protective regulation. This regulation was originally intended to protect those who invested huge sums in a capital-intensive business and to ensure that they had enough opportunity to recuperate their original investment in the absence of stifling competitive pressure. In many cases these investors were the populations of the world's nations through the auspices of their domestic governments. The problem, as with many policies, is that the protective shell of economic regulation became an end unto itself. Regulation grew to a point where it began to remove the opportunities that many investors desired to enhance the position of their carrier, in which they had invested heavily. Now that the job of building the system is complete, for now, it seems a propitious time to allow its cultivated market players to go out into the market and compete. While the air transport infrastructure is under the pressure of excessive utilization, the replacement or renewal of these facilities can be done gradually thus avoiding the huge single cash infusion that was required to build the system in the first place. With innovative management taking a leading role in determining the future winners and losers among air transport corporations, it seems natural that bigger and bigger carriers will evolve. The arrival of an air transport multinational will find its way into the system. This type of carrier structure may be composed of stake-holders from many nations but it will operate as a single cohesive airline unit. It will also have the best chance of being able to afford the coming technological revolution. We stand on the horizon of exciting times as did the Wright brothers or Juan Trippe or Lindbergh or any of our other air heroes. That is, of course, one of the most exciting things about air transportation: it is always challenging in a different way. We also find ourselves at the early maturity stage of the science of airline management; we are poised to discover supersonic strategies or the widebodies of efficient strategic thinking. The future seems to hold a golden era of airline management followed by the second coming of the golden age of technological advancement and the hypersonic generation.

5 Strategic management applications

'The predictive value of accurate strategic thinking is rarely accepted until it becomes conventional wisdom by which time it has, of course, diminished in value.' [40]

Within most modern airlines the importance of good non-technical management skills is a relatively new concept. After all, we are still feeling the 'halo effect' of the larger and faster technology aircraft developed in the 1960s and early 1970s. As such, the golden age of strategic airline management lies ahead, as opposed to behind us. We cannot expect a significant efficiency boost from the technological side until the second generation of supersonic or even hypersonic aircraft are developed and flying in regular commercial service. Many of the so-called new designs that are scheduled to enter into service in the next five years are evolutionary technology as opposed to revolutionary technology. How then are the airlines of the world going to fight the immense competitive battles that lie ahead? Factors such as sensitivity to competition, advanced strategic planning, strong product marketing, the constant fight to improve the consistent quality of customer service, cost restraint combined paradoxically with innovative asset acquisition and management, among other factors, will become the new determinants of success. We have already seen the kind of scenario evolve whereby the new corporate heroes are the ones that negotiate a successful takeover, bring out a new product and launch it properly or are part of a competent group of customer service employees. Privatization, deregulation or liberalization and the *status quo* technical nature of current generation aircraft have left airline management groups with practically the full weight of generating productive innovation within their corporate infrastructure. This is at once an exciting and terrifying prospect. The US airline group illustrated that new found commercial independence is often accompanied by its share of errors. Carriers affected by various other subsequent liberalizations and deregulations should benefit from the experience of watching US carrier reactions but will of course find more than a few occasions on which to make their own seemingly original errors. Part and parcel of making mistakes is the hope that one will also have a higher proportion of successes. As human beings we have an inherent dislike of excessive change, especially the kind that is unexpected or comes faster than expected. This is compounded in the air transport business by a simultaneous shifting of the burden of innovation away from the technical side onto the backs of the management group.

Are there any tools, methods or processes that can help corporations to enjoy the benefits and innovation that flow from a sound strategic planning mechanism? The answer is a qualified yes and each major carrier probably has its own, which is the ideal configuration for its particular circumstances. The issue is that many carriers will be forced to change their way of doing things in order to better adapt to the new competitive realities.

Strategic basics

Planning cycles, like the economy, have their own rhythm (see Fig. 5.1). During rough financial times most companies try to concentrate on tomorrow morning or next week but are certainly not interested in anything remotely perceived as long term. The low ebb of a carrier's

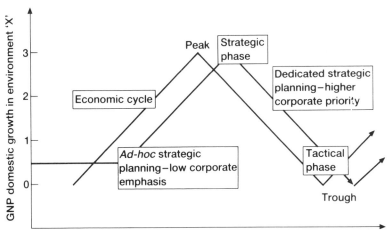

Figure 5.1 **Strategic planning cycles**

financial health tends to parallel the tactical phase of their management cycle. Matching the lowest prevailing price in key markets, cutting costs, rationalizing the service standards in the product, cutting back on frequency of operation, all tend to be short-term solutions that are eventually modified or even reversed when things start to improve. During this time, low priority is assigned to planning and it tends to be a relatively *ad-hoc* activity that is carried out when all the other 'today oriented crises' have been resolved. Tactical management makes sense in this phase because there is little or no new growth in the market. Consequently the skills required are those that produce a superior ability to steal market share from competitors. Lower price, more frequent flier bonus points, advertising and a higher proportion of no-frills type product tend to attract the ultra-price-sensitive consumers that make up an important proportion of the total market in any recessionary phase.

Once the imminent crises have passed, then airline management groups feel less guilty about devoting some time to planning for the future. In many cases detailed long-term plans are developed and then systematically modified as reality overtakes the plan. Recognizing this inherent tendency to do different types of planning in the various phases is not enough. There is a strong disincentive towards strategic planning in most corporations simply because the implicit criteria for judgement of performance are also based on a relatively short-term basis. Airline management groups are rarely rewarded for pursuing money-losing strategies even if they turn in a profit, on schedule, in the second year. That is because the reward system in airlines, as in most corporations, tends to be short-term. The amusing thing about deregulation is that it has created even more of a short-term mentality. In a very competitive environment where the extremes are dizzying success, ultimate bankruptcy or a corporate take over, one tends to try and stay strong in the short term because otherwise there may not be a long term.

Why must the tactical and the strategic be separate activities that almost seem at cross-purposes with each other? After all, the quality of strategic projection during a previous economic cycle will go a long way towards determining the quality of life for the tactician in the following cycle. The fact that Northwest had kept its labour costs low and had a meticulous financial planning discipline made it one of the better prepared carriers for deregulation. Conversely, the fact that Eastern did not have low labour costs nor a particularly good financial background or a distinctive strategic direction meant that they would probably have more difficulty during deregulation. Air transport industry management groups don't start planning for the upturn or peak of the economic cycle until they are more than halfway through it. They don't realize that it is time to start consolidating until the income statement states that a large loss has either occurred or is projected for the next 6 months. The strategy behind a successful consolidation is as important as the planning for growth. In fact the need for sound strategic planning is continuous even if the objective of that strategic planning will modify itself as all airlines travel along the roller-coaster path of the economic cycle. Accurate strategic planning serves as an early warning system for both the threatening or potentially profitable phenomena that may affect the corporation. It also allows competing airlines to differentiate themselves by acting on what they believe are innovative and profitable strategies before other carriers. After a successful innovation has been installed at one carrier, many others will copy it. Defining a clear and simple process to handle these critical factors within an airline is still a rather unsophisticated process at many carriers.

Airlines have a basic simple function which is the transportation of people and goods, thus providing the benefit of timely transit. In providing this service, carriers, composed of people and machines, try to evolve the most efficient, highest quality structure to perform this task. Finding the correct balance between machines and people is a complex issue, as is finding the right number of machines and people to serve the carriers' needs at various phases of the economic cycle. The problem is that we cannot put people and aircraft in a cupboard during a recession until they are again needed in the next upturn and peak of the market cycle.

The service provided is aimed at consumers who are grouped into markets. It may be soundly argued that in the early days, when people and freight were used to travelling at a rather slower pace, airlines had to create a need among consumers. This is, of course, no longer the case. The calamity that ensues from a strike by a major carrier is ample proof of the perceived consumer need for air transportation. Trying to continously serve this dynamic consumer service requirement is another very tricky thing to do. An additional complication that arises is the fact that other competitors seem to think that they can better address these dynamic consumer needs. In addition, a certain amount of consumer conditioning has made the optimization of airline missions more difficult. The feeling in many markets, especially those that have been deregulated or liberalized, is that a low fare is the only fare worth travelling on. Over 90 per cent of

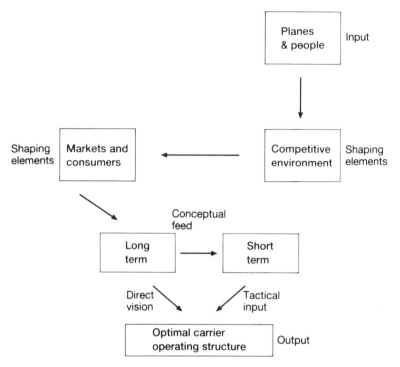

Figure 5.2 **Planning factors of production**

all US air travel is now on some kind of a discount fare, even though 54 per cent of all travel in the US is still by business travellers, a group that used to generate high yield not discount fare returns. After the airlines and the government have extolled the virtues of a deregulation, the net message to the consumer is that it will cost less. This has caused a Pavlovian response to low fare offers and a reticence to travel in other periods. In fact, a very low fare may even create a need in consumers to travel that would not otherwise have occurred. The fact that in most countries the increases in air fares have consistently been below the consumer price index increases since the 1940s would tend to support the feeling that air travel should not cost much. An additional factor that tends to make people feel that they may not have achieved significant value for their money is the fact that air travel is, of course, an intangible service. One rents a seat for a period of time. In order to cope with the dynamism of consumers and that of the other market competitors, all airlines develop short- and long-term strategies and tactics. All of the above are conditioned and complicated by an inevitable dose of change. The more the pace of change quickens the more the equation becomes complicated. Airlines use three basic lines of defence to answer the challenge.

Diagnostic Generics

For every carrier there are common generic factors that can be analysed and diagnosed in determining carrier health. What are these specific elements that influence the critical structure of a carrier? How does one keep score on the level of success for a specific carrier? Traditional methods include profit and loss, traffic growth, yield improvement, market share, better performance parameters for product delivery, or some other comparable measure. Inevitably these results are reflections of how a bundle of other variables are performing. Figure 5.3 denotes those criteria that separated carriers into distinct groups in the US post-deregulation environment. The carriers that tended to have the best composite scores in each area were the ones recognized as the market leaders. The difficulty is in attaching a relative weight to each variable. For example, while US Air was one of the highest cost carriers of any in the US it still managed very respectable financial returns. In this case US Air was able to maximize its hub pattern, network mass in smaller markets and its market share in these less competitive and therefore higher yield markets. US Air was also the first carrier to use commuter feed agreements to direct grass-roots feed to its jet network (see US Air/ Piedmont carrier strategy). The art of accurate diagnostics is invaluable because it forms the basis for tactical and strategic action. A specifically tailored strategic tool will also allow an accurate assessment of the strengths and weaknesses of competitors. Diagnostic activity is the only relatively secure management activity since it is a description of the past. Performance is usually measured in two ways:

(1) against that of previous periods or

(2) versus that of the competition.

By looking at the diagnostic factors (Fig. 5.3), a carrier can be graded as either a type 1 (high-cost, full-service), type 2 (low-cost, low-service) or a type 3 (low-cost, medium or differentiated service levels). Placing a carrier in the context of one of the three types and then doing the same for the market competitors will provide a relatively clear picture of the differences and any options to improve its position that might be required.

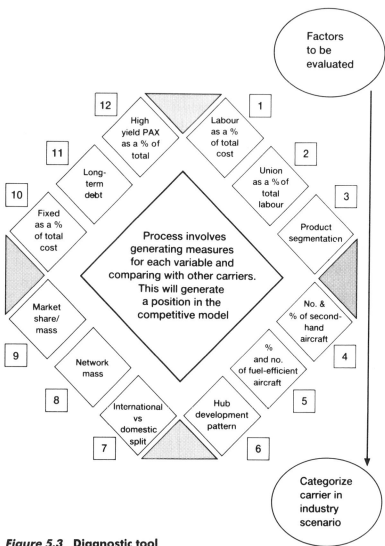

Figure 5.3 **Diagnostic tool**

Environmental modelling

Once the critical characteristics of a carrier and those of the competition have been diagnosed, then trying to find a simple and workable expression of that environment becomes the next step. As illustrated in Chapters 2 and 3, the modelling of the environment will lead strategists to a superior ability to not only recognize the competition and their strengths and weaknesses but also to project how these strengths and weaknesses will evolve through the economic cycle. Various domestic environments and the international air transport marketplace each have different competitive characteristics. There is a link between each, however. Clearly the deregulation of the US environment has had ripple effects in many environments, both domestic and international. The beauty of a deregulation is that air transport becomes like any other business which means that strategic models can be borrowed from other industries. The automobile business has its own equivalents to the type 1, 2 and 3 carrier types, as do the computer, steel, electronics and other industries. The critical common elements in any modelling exercise are the development of a series of contrasting company characteristics that differentiate the competitors in a given market. Usually two or three different or segmented corporate structures will emerge, each of which will tend to exhibit different tendencies in a common environment (e.g. low cost and volume oriented, or high cost, high quality, high yield and lower volume oriented). Each type of carrier should represent a fundamentally different corporate philosophy. Once one has determined these various types within a given environment, then the projection of the tendencies of each type at various phases of the economic cycle will produce the timing pattern which will govern future moments of opportunity or, conversely, consolidation for each market player.

Once this plan is developed, adequately communicated and installed throughout the entire corporate environment, then an airline will become less surprised at change and will have developed a longer term vision of itself and its evolution within the various marketplaces that it serves. Instead of looking at each future day or month, the future becomes a more predictable piece of a cyclical puzzle. As a result, as seen in Chapter 2, the strategist can begin to predict when to buy, lease or sell fleet, increase or liquidate debt, expand or contract market activities, consolidate operations and cut costs or project a host of other variables that help keep an airline's own structure at harmony with the current magnitude of its transportation task. As such this qualitatively based methodology seeks to get airlines away from a reliance on inherently inaccurate statistically generated quantitative projections that many carriers ignore as soon as they are produced. The key thought is to enhance predictability and reduce unexpected surprises in operating an airline in a dynamic and sometimes hostile competitive environment.

Airline asset acquisition and disposal

A key subcomponent of future success is the projection or strategic vision regarding asset acquisition/disposal. Carriers traditionally attempt to vary the value and quantity of the assets of which they dispose in order to maximize the incremental revenue gains implicit in the peak/upturn of the market cycle. Similarly most carriers try to reduce assets in the trough/downturn of the cycle in order to save costs.

In order to be more efficient and cost effective, unfortunately, as was seen in the chapter on the US, this cyclical asset management strategy is more easily said than done. Aircraft and human resource piles have traditionally had low flexibility attached to them. A second complicating factor is that management's corrective action, to conform to cyclical movement, usually lags behind the actual cycle by months, if not more. As a result some carriers have sought to stabilize this matter by maintaining a relatively constant approach to asset acquisition and disposal. While most carriers grow their asset base as they expand, the pace of asset growth does differentiate carriers from

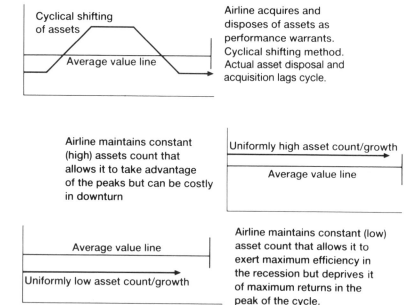

Figure 5.4 **Airline asset acquisition and asset deployment strategies. (Asset refers to aircraft/human and other resource piles.)**

each other. In fact, some carriers adopt an intentionally conservative approach which calls for slow asset growth and therefore a uniformly lower asset growth quotient. This means that these conservative carriers are more efficient in the trough/downturn: conversely, more risk-prone carriers do the opposite and indulge in a more liberal approach. These liberal carriers have a higher incremental revenue gain in the peak than their conservative brethren. No matter which approach is adopted, the timely management of assets will continue to be a key to success for the airlines. The optimal result would be to match assets to market needs. Aircraft leasing, part-time employment and other related resource strategies attempt to provide carriers with flexibility. The more flexibility the better the ability and speed of adjusting assets to market dictates.

The golden rules

As we saw in Chapter 2, many US carriers who had developed their own set of golden rules soon found out that many of these had changed due to the newly deregulated US air transport market. That taught a single lesson that golden rules are not necessarily cast in stone, which means that they cannot be static golden rules. There are, however, some relatively commonsense rules or guidelines which can serve as a general guide. For example, as regards the area of fleet, one could advise that in an economic trough period the number of types should be streamlined to as few as possible. This reduces maintenance and training costs while allowing maximum interchangeability of aircraft to cater to varying route volume requirements. Aircraft fleets should be obtainable and disposable factors of production. Fleet management now requires a more flexible approach than ever before, keeping aircraft for the sake of keeping them until the next market peak is a luxury few can afford any more. Finally, the timing of fleet purchases is critical. Most new aircraft should be delivered during the upturn of the economic cycle not after the peak. Because many carriers acquire the funding to buy new aircraft during the best economic period and then place the order for new aircraft, they inevitably take delivery when they can least afford to make the payments.

As regards route networks, the optimal nature of a route system should always be recognized. Simply saying one had a hub was not enough for Delta; Piedmont proved that second-generation hubs, with higher quality and more reliable transit facilities were a superior configuration, and consumers agreed with this assessment. Today, a multiple hub operation may be the state-of-the-art configuration. Any given US domestic carrier must have a web of big, medium and mini-hubs interwoven by a high-frequency route network to develop adequate market mass. What will be next? In developing larger hubs, carriers are bound to make mistakes. The ability to go into and then out of a market should not be ignored because of potential embarrassment. There is no point in staying in a losing market when these funds could be re-deployed elsewhere for new more profitable growth. Finally, in the new market realities of today, carriers can no longer permit themselves to use operational constraints as the key planning criteria for route network development. The optimization of consumers' needs must take priority.

The area of human resource management has obviously undergone gigantic change. The words deregulation or liberalization mean one thing to employees, be they union or non-union: more work and relatively less money. The intense competitive environment means that longer hours become more commonplace among management staff and more flexible job tasks are common to all. The use of part-time labour, job sharing and various other softer methods of productivity improvement become the rule as opposed to the exception. The trauma that these changes cause should not be underestimated. It is clear that change affects all. It is more important than ever for all components to do their jobs well. The 'us-*vs*-them' attitude that prevails between organized labour and management is no longer a realistic option for a successful carrier to contemplate. The synergy of all must equal a sum greater than the parts. In the highly socialistic Scandinavian countries, we have witnessed the abrupt change at SAS that has been predicated on letting every individual do his or her primary job, which is serving the customer. Many who were along for the ride have found the airline business a somewhat less comfortable sector to be in these days. Those who stay and are part of increasing their carrier's success probably feel a greater sense of achievement. How can carriers facilitate this good feeling among their employees? A variety of methods have been used and the following list is by no means an exhaustive one. The first concept many try to install in their employees' minds is that automatic remuneration regardless of performance is simply no longer a possible option. Therefore, a whole slew of incentive-based employee stock-ownership plans, profit-sharing plans and other similar instruments have been developed to reward what the airline needs most, competent performance. A change in management culture, that great undefinable controller of corporate activity, usually means an improved efficiency in decision-making processes. At SAS this meant that in many cases the front-line customer service employee had more discretion to do his or her job to maximize customer service. The redistribution of perceived power is a very tricky subset of the changes brought on by a modified decision-making system, the ramifications of which should not be overlooked. Part and parcel of modified decision-making streams is the development of an increased sense of pride in all employees and a sense of greater responsibility for the corporate good at all levels. Instead of guaranteed remuneration employees feel challenged to work and get involved. Overall, the air transport business is tougher for employees to work within and, while automatic remuneration is no longer optimal, frequent recognition of outstanding performance should help replace the diminished future security of working in a deregulated industry sector.

Given the dynamic nature of the market, there would not seem to be any guidelines that are applicable at all times. One can develop a set of guidelines for each major airline component. There should be two variations on these guidelines which are conditioned by whether a carrier is in the upturn and peak or downturn and pit of the applicable economic cycle.

In conclusion, the application of new strategic methods forms the foundation stone upon which the ability to deal effectively with change will be predicated. The better the strategic planning, the more warning a carrier has and the better the quality of its reaction to adversity. Airlines should not be afraid to embrace change; instead, carriers should try to absorb productive dynamism into their structure faster and with more success than their competitors can.

6 Conclusions

'Not more than five of the European airlines will survive as major intercontinental carriers' Jan Carlzon, Chief Executive, SAS, 1987

One of the things that has impressed me about many of the people that I have had the good fortune to come in contact with through my air transportation-oriented teaching and consulting activities has been the general and continuing disbelief that significant change would ever fundamentally alter the industry. During the late 1970s and even in the early 1980s, many still thought that deregulation in the US would not work. Several predictions for re-regulation have surfaced at various times and this is again a current topic in the US. The huge body of airline managers who were trained to improve their market position by dealing through the regulators, as opposed to the consumer, appear bewildered. Now that the impacts of US deregulation have become conventional topics of discussion, we find the same resistance to a phenomenon of international liberalization and the evolution of global air carriers. When I first wrote about the multimega carrier, in mid-1986 (a year before the current furore), raising the spectre of a 'Royal-Ameripore Airlines', many thought these were amusing anecdotes at best. Many carriers are busy denying that they are involved with any such scheme although recent industry activity indicated that most are talking about some form of alliance/joint venture with at least one other carrier. It becomes difficult to deny that air transportation is not evolving into an industry sector just like any other. The current attachment between national pride and the operation of a flag carrier will eventually wither away for the right price. Many never thought that the strategically important computer business or other huge industrial sectors could ever be left to free market forces with a potential for majority foreign ownership, but this has happened. As the expansion of free-trade zones, common customs unions and the GATT (General Agreement on Trade and Tariffs) evolve, the tendency seems to be towards a freer global attitude to trade. There is every chance that air transportation could become embroiled in this freer market access mentality. Some carriers are already proposing that all international air bilateral rights be replaced by a most-favoured nation trade (that would reduce market access barriers) system similar to that of GATT. Invariably these carriers come from smaller countries, like Holland, that have very little to lose and everything to gain in this kind of system, because they have virtually no domestic markets of their own for others to exploit.

While the dismantling of the air bilateral system may never occur, the current trends towards air carrier alliance, joint ventures and the construction of multimega carriers can continue within a minimally modified air bilateral system. Commercial innovation will lead regulatory change in the future.

In conclusion I would make some fearless (or is that fearful?) predictions for the future of the industry that those of us who work within it have come to know and love (see Fig. 6.1).

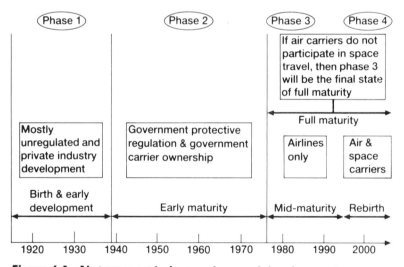

Figure 6.1 **Air transport industry phases of development**

The one constant in the life of all airline managers will be change. As the industry moves into the next phase of its maturity process, airlines will become more like companies in other industries. The ultimate symbol of commercial success will be the multimega air carrier. There will be far fewer major airlines in the world by 1992 than there are today. As Mr J. Carlzon of SAS said in the 24 and 25 Sept. 1987 issue of *Aviation Daily*: 'It makes no sense, necessarily, for an American to fly on a US airline and a Scandinavian to fly on a Scandinavian airline. Aviation is moving into being a global business venture ...If you look upon this as a pure business proposal, then you can raise yourself above the nationalistic links. But if you begin with nationalistic links and try to form a business proposal, it is going to become much more difficult.' In an industry that is already noted for its rather low average returns on investment, it will be harder to make a profit due to tougher competition. This may lead air carriers to become part of diversified multinational conglomerates whereby the cross-fertilization of skills between the different industry sectors may improve ROIs. The airline industry will continue to see an influx of managers that are sound generic marketers, strategists, financiers etc. as it adopts more non-airline-specific attitudes towards corporate development. In fact the trend of outside managers and chief executives coming into air transportation has already been observed at many airlines, as have the beginnings of multinational conglomerate interest in obtaining airline holdings. The years between 1978 and 1998 will become known as the late-maturity phase of the air transport business as we know it today.

Beyond the late 1990s air transportation will either stagnate at the conventional air transport level while a whole series of new space-travel carriers evolve into a separate mode of transportation, or it will be preparing to enter a whole new era of travel technology. If the latter occurs, these air/space carriers will either require government funding which may lead to some de-privatizations or even some form of protective route regulation that will allow carriers, who make these huge investments, to have an adequate opportunity to recuperate their investments. Does that sound familiar?

In the interim, as one stands back and looks at the past 60 years of air transportation, it becomes clear that the next 20 years will be just as exciting if not more so. The age of aircraft technology will be followed by the age of management technology and the scope for significant achievement will remain undiminished. Developing and implementing a strong and distinctive corporate strategic thrust (or vision) while making sure that all the employees of a given airline not only understand but support it will become critical. Dealing with and consistently pleasing the consumer in a variety of distinct global markets will be the critical priority for all carriers around the world modulated only by the cyclical conditioners of market preference. Finally, it is hoped that new methods such as some of those outlined in previous chapters will aid the manager, students and others in trying to take some of the unpredictability out of the future planning process.

Notes

1. *The Airline Builders*, Time Life, Alexandria, Virginia, p. 17.
2. Meyer/Oster/Morgan /Berman/Strassman, *Airline Deregulation, The Early Experience*, p. 13.
3. *The Airline Builders, op. cit.*, p. 19.
4. *Ibid.*, p. 24.
5. *Ibid.*
6. Payne, L.G.S., *Air Dates*, Toronto, p. 39.
7. *The Airline Builders, op cit.*, p. 52.
8. *Ibid.*, p. 52.
9. *Ibid.*, pp. 52–3.
10. Taneja, N.K., *The Commercial Airline Industry*, Lexington Books, p. 1.
11. *Regulation and Competition in Air Transportation*, Richmond, p. 4.
12. *Commerical Airline Industry, op. cit.*, p. 12.
13. *Regulation and Competition, op. cit.*, p. 4.
14. *Commercial Airline Industry, op. cit.*, p. 2.
15. *Regulation and Competition, op. cit.*, p. 6.
16. *Ibid.*
17. *Ibid.*
18. *Commercial Airline Industry, op. cit.*, p. 5.
19. Institute of Air and Space Law, *Casebook – Government Regulation of Air Transportation, 1981–82*, McGill University, p. 743.
20. *Ibid.*
21. *Ibid.*, p. 744.
22. 'Rumblings of re-regulation', Staff Article, *Fortune Magazine*, 10 January 1983, p. 17.
23. *Ibid.*, pp. 17–18.
24. *Airline Deregulation, op cit.*, p. 35.
25. *Ibid.*, p. 26.
26. *Ibid.*, p. 32.
27. *Ibid.*
28. McIntosh, C.H., *Air Transport World*, June 1976, p. 50.
29. *Ibid.*
30. *Airline Deregulation, op. cit.*, p. 36.
31. *Ibid.*
32. *Ibid.*, p. 37.
33. 'Kahn Urging CAB Deregulation Drive', *AW & ST*, 6 March 1978, p. 35.
34. Robertson, T.S., Ward, S., *Management Lessons from Airline Deregulation*, *HBR*, Jan–Feb. 1983, p. 41.

35. Airline Industry Seminar, *Facing the Challenges of Dereguation*, Lehman Brothers, Kuhn Loeb Research, p. 7.
36. Details drawn from 'The Final Frontier', *Frequent Flyer Magazine*, March 1987, pp. 64–75.
37. *Ibid.*, p. 72.
38. *Ibid.*, p. 70.
39. Gialloreto, L., 'European Deregulation and the Coming of the Multimega Carrier', Avmark European Aviation Conference, Venice, 1987.
40. Gialloreto, L., 'The Role of European Airlines in the World of the Multimega Carrier, Profit versus Politics', 3rd Annual Avmark Conference on European Aviation, Paris, 1988.

Bibliography

Volumes

Air Transport Association of America, *Annual Reports*, for 1955, 1957, 1958, 1978–87.

Air Transport Association of Canada, *Annual Report*, 1982.

Allen, O.E., (ed.), *The Airline Builders*, Time-Life Books, Alexandra, Virginia, 1981

Canadian Transport Commission: Research Branch, *Transport Review – Trends and Selected Issues – 1981*.

An Analysis of ATC Decisions – 1973–78.

A Productivity Study of the Canadian Airline Industry.

Carlzon, J., *Moments of Truth*, Ballinger Publishing, Cambridge, 1987.

Davies, R.E.G., *A History of the World's Airlines*, Oxford University Press, Toronto, 1964.

Galbraith, J.K., *A Theory of Price Control*, Harvard University Press, Cambridge, 1952.

IATA, Act of Incorporation, Articles of Association and the Rules and Regulations. IATA, Montreal, Canada.

ICAO Circulars, *Handbook on Administrative Clauses in Bilateral Air Transport Agreements* (63-AT/6), (72-AT/9), ICAO, Montreal, Canada.

Institute of Air and Space Law, McGill University, *Casebook in Government Regulation*, Montreal, Quebec, 1982.

Jordan, W.A., *Performance of Regulated Canadian Airlines in Domestic and Transborder Operations*, Consumer and Corporate Affairs, Ottawa, Ontario, 1983.

Kirk, R., *An Airline Fare Structure for Tomorrow,* Transport Research Forum, Vol. 18, No. 1, 1979.

Lehman Brothers, Kuhn Loeb Research, *Facing the Challenges of Deregulation* (Airline Industry Seminar), New York, Feb. 1982.

Meyer, Oster, Morgan, Berman, Strassman, *Airline Deregulation, the Early Experience*, Auburn House Publishing Co., Boston, 1981.

Reschentaler, G.B. and Roberts, B. (eds), *Perspectives on Canadian Airline Regulation*, Butterworth & Co. (Canada) Ltd, Montreal, 1979.

Richmond, S.B., *Regulation and Competition in Air Transportation*, Columbia University Press, New York, 1961.

Spencer, F.A., *A Reappraisal of Transport Aircraft Needs 1985–2000* (prepared for NASA), Northwestern University, Chicago, Jan. 1982.

Taneja, N.K., *The Commercial Airline Industry,* Lexington Books (D.C. Heath & Co.), Toronto, 1976.

Tugendhat, C., *The Multinationals*, Penguin Books, Middlesex, UK, 1971.

Whitehouse, A., *The Sky's the Limit*, Macmillan & Co., New York, 1971.

Wyckoff, O.D. and Maister, P.H., *The Domestic Airline Industry*, Lexington Books (D.C. Heath & Co.), Toronto, 1977.

Documents

Air Transport Asssociation of America, Annual Reports 1978–87
European Economic Community:

Treaty of Rome, Arts. 85, 86 and 92.
European Parliament Working Documents, June 1982, Doc. 1–286/82/GORR.
EC Bulletin, 7/8, 1981, pp. 15–17.
Commission of European Communities, Council Regulation, COM(81) 396 Final.
Bulletin of European Communities, Supp., 5179, 'Air Transport: A Community Approach'.

Ministry of Transport (Canada), Press Releases 7 Nov. 1978, 14 Aug. 1981.

Speakers' papers for the 1st Airline Management Development Association Conference, *Deregulated Airline Thinking*, Montreal, May 1987.
Speakers' papers for the 7th Lloyds International Civil Aviation Conference, The Hague, 24–25 October 1985, Lloyds of London Press, New York, 1985.

Periodicals

Airline Business, following editions:

August 1987
September 1987
October 1987
November 1987
December 1987

Airline Executive, following editions:

November 1982
January 1983

Air Transport World, following editions:

June 1976
June 1977
October 1977
November 1977
January 1978
May 1978
June 1978
July 1978
August 1978
September 1978
October 1978
December 1978
January 1979
April 1979
July 1979
August 1979
November 1979
December 1979
January 1980

May 1980
June 1980
October 1980
December 1980
April 1981
May 1981
June 1981
August 1981
September 1981
March 1983
May 1986
June 1986
June 1987

Aviation Daily, following editions:

16, 23 April 1982
23 June 1982
19, 28 July 1982
23 August 1982
24 September 1982
12, 28 October 1982
9, 10, 15, 28 February 1983
1, 2, 3, 4, 7, 8, 9, 10, 14, 16 March 1983
All issues for 1986 and 1987

Aviation Week and Space Technology, following editions:

6, 20 March 1978
16, 30 August 1982
24 January 1983
28 February 1983
7 March 1983
All 1987 editions

Avmark Aviation Economist, all editions

Business Week, following editions:

8, 15 November 1982
13, 27 December 1982
7, 14, 28 February 1983
4, 18, 25 April 1983
2, 16 March 1987

27 April 1987
22 June 1987
14, 22, 28 September 1987
5 October 1987

Canadian Aviation, following editions:

February 1983
April 1983

Canadian Business, following editions:

February 1982
March 1983

Canadian Travel Press, following edition:

November 1982

The Economist, following editions:

13 November 1982
4 December 1982
15 January 1983
5, 26 February 1983
12, 26 March 1983
16 April 1983

Flight International, following editions:

10, 17, 24 June 1978
15 July 1978
9, 23 September 1978
25 November 1978
21, 28 April 1979
26 May 1979
30 June 1979
14 July 1979
10 November 1979
8, 22 December 1979
5 January 1980
2, 9, 16 February 1980
6 December 1980
27 February 1982
9 October 1982

20 November 1982
4 December 1982
1, 8 January 1982
12 February 1982
5, 26 March 1982
9, 16 April 1983

Fortune Magazine, following editions:

29 November 1982
10 January 1983
11, 25 May 1987
7 December 1987

Frequent Flyer Magazine, following editions:

May 1987
August 1987
September 1987

Howard Business Review, following editions:

July–August 1982
January–February 1983

ITA Magazine, following editions:

July/August 1987

Interavia, following edition:

February 1983

Lloyds Aviation Economist, all editions from 1985

US News and World Report, following editions:

13, 20 December 1982
21 March 1983

Newspapers

The Montreal Gazette, 24 February 1983.
The Washington Post, 31 October 1982.
The New York Times, 3 April 1983.

Index